A Will Is Not Enough
In Pennsylvania

SIMPLE, PRACTICAL THINGS
A PENNSYLVANIA RESIDENT CAN DO TO

- ❖ PRESERVE ASSETS
- ❖ AVOID PROBATE
- ❖ AVOID GUARDIANSHIP
- ❖ PROVIDE FOR HEALTH CARE
- ❖ PROVIDE FOR THE FAMILY'S CARE

By AMELIA E. POHL, ESQ.
and
Pennsylvania Attorney
ANTHONY R. FANTINI

EAGLE PUBLISHING COMPANY OF BOCA

Copyright © 2003 by AMELIA E. POIIL
All rights reserved.
No part of this book may be reproduced or transmitted for any purpose, in any form and by any means, graphic, electronic or mechanical, including photocopying, recording, or by any information storage or retrieval system, without permission in writing from AMELIA E. POHL.

The purpose of this book is to provide the reader with an informative overview of the subject; but laws change frequently and are subject to different interpretations as courts rule on the meaning or effect of a law. This book is sold with the understanding that the publisher and the authors are not engaging in, or rendering legal, accounting, medical, psychiatric, financial planning or any other professional service. If you need legal, accounting, medical, psychiatric, financial planning or other expert advice, then you should seek the services of a licensed professional.

This book is intended for use by the consumer for his or her own benefit. If you use this book to counsel someone about the law or tax matters, then that may be considered to be an unauthorized and illegal practice.

WEB SITES: Web sites appear throughout the book. These Web sites are offered for the convenience of the reader only. Publication of these Web site addresses is not an endorsement by the authors, editors or publishers of this book.

EAGLE PUBLISHING COMPANY OF BOCA
4199 N. Dixie Highway, #2
Boca Raton, FL   33431   E-mail: info@eaglepublishing.com

Printed in the United States of America
ISBN 1-892407-77-9
Library of Congress Catalog Card Number: 2002112284

Introduction

Over the years, as we practiced law, we noticed that the questions people have about Wills, Trusts, powers of attorney, avoiding probate and guardianship, preserving assets, providing health care for themselves and their families, are much the same client to client. Many people are concerned about who will control their finances should they become too aged or too ill to do so themselves. Of even more concern is their health care:

Who will make my medical decisions if I can't do so myself?
How can I pay for my health care?
How much and what type of insurance should I have?
How can I avoid guardianship?

Others worry about the care of family members. Those with minor children worry:

Who will care for my minor child if I become incapacitated or die?

Is there a way to make sure my child has enough money to see him through college?

Those with elderly parents worry:

How can I manage my parent's finances should my parent become too aged or ill to do so?

Can my parent qualify for MEDICAID?

If my parent dies, will I need to go through Probate?

Is there a way to avoid Probate?

We agreed that a book answering such questions would be of service to the general public. We wish to thank all of the clients, whom we have had the honor and pleasure to serve, for providing us with the impetus to write this book.

Anthony R. Fantini

ANTHONY R. FANTINI is the founder of the FANTINI LAW FIRM, P.C. The Fantini Law Firm is known to be one of high character, professionalism, and a strong commitment to client satisfaction. Even more important is the integrity, attitude, and dedication to their profession found in everyone who works at The Fantini Law Firm.

The Fantini Law Firm is located in Pittsburgh, and has clients throughout Western Pennsylvania.

Mr. Fantini concentrates on issues of Elder Law, Estate Planning, Asset Protection and Business transition. He makes practical and effective Estate Planning tools available to his clients. He puts his extensive experience to use in preparing understandable, pragmatic, estate plans for his clients.

Anthony R. Fantini is licensed to practice before the United States Tax Court, the Supreme Court of the Commonwealth of Pennsylvania and the Western Pennsylvania Federal District Court. He is a member of the National Academy of Elder Law Attorneys.

Mr. Fantini regularly presents continuing education classes for other professional advisors such as Certified Public Accountants, Financial Planners and Insurance Agents.

Anthony R. Fantini belongs to the AMERICAN ACADEMY OF ESTATE PLANNING ATTORNEYS and regularly provides free educational seminars to the community on the subject of Estate Planning.

About the Academy

The American Academy of Estate Planning Attorneys is a member organization serving the needs of legal professionals concentrating on Estate Planning. Through the Academy's comprehensive training and educational programs on state-of-the-art Estate Planning law and techniques, it fosters excellence in Estate Planning among its members and helps them deliver the highest possible service to their clients. The Academy provides its members with excellent legal education, and top notch practice management support. In addition, each member is required to attain thirty-six units of continuing legal education annually.

The American Academy of Estate Planning Attorneys serves law firms in over 150 geographic areas in forty-four states. Clients who chose an attorney who is a member of the Academy can feel confident that they have an attorney who is dedicated to bringing them the highest quality of service.

The Academy is also committed to educating consumers on vital Estate Planning issues that touch their lives. Through its series of publications, educational programs and its consumer Web site, the Academy seeks to create a public armed with the information they need to become wise consumers of Estate Planning services.

 THE AMERICAN ACADEMY OF ESTATE PLANNING ATTORNEYS WEB SITE
http://www.aaepa.com

Amelia E. Pohl, Esq.

Before becoming an attorney in 1985, AMELIA E. POHL taught mathematics on both the high school and college level. During her tenure as Associate Professor of Mathematics at Prince George's Community College in Maryland, she wrote several books including Probability: A Set Theory Approach, Principals of Counting and Common Stock Sense.

During her practice of law Attorney Pohl observed that many people want to reduce the high cost of legal fees by performing or assisting with their own legal transactions.

Attorney Pohl found that, with a bit of guidance, people are able to perform many legal transactions for themselves. Attorney Pohl utilizes her background as teacher, author and attorney to provide that "bit of guidance" to the general public in the form of self-help legal books that she has written. Because there is such variation in the laws from state to state, each book written by Attorney Pohl is state specific.

Amelia Pohl is currently "translating" this book for the remaining states with the assistance of an attorney from each state who is licensed to practice in the given state.

Call EAGLE PUBLISHING COMPANY OF BOCA at (800) 824-0823 to learn of the availability of this book for any other state.

Acknowledgment

Special thanks to Pennsylvania attorney HAROLD N. FLIEGELMAN for his review of the Medicaid section of this book (Chapters 10 and 11) for compliance with Pennsylvania law.

Mr. Fliegelman is the founder of FLIEGELMAN ELDERLAW, a law firm located in Norristown, Pennsylvania that deals exclusively with the legal problems of older and disabled people. The firm's special focus is on preserving client's assets from the devastating financial demands of health care costs and nursing homes.

Mr. Fliegelman is the author of *Medicaid Planning For Guardians*, published by the Law Review of the Wake Forest University School of Law. He also served as Consulting Counsel on the publication *Guiding Those Left Behind in Pennsylvania*. Mr. Fliegelman also writes and publishes a monthly newsletter entitled ELDERLAW.

Mr. Fliegelman is also the owner and operator of ELDER PLANNING SERVICES, LLC, an Internet provider services to Medicaid Planning professionals. You can find more information about these services on the Internet.
http://www.elderps.com

Reading the Law

Where applicable, we identified the state statute or federal statute that is the basis of the discussion. We did this as a reference, and also to encourage the reader to look at the law as it is written. Prior to the Internet the only way you could look up the law was to physically take yourself to the local courthouse law library or the law section of a public library. Today state and federal statutes are literally at your finger tips. They are just a mouse click away on the Internet. To look up a statute all you need is the address of the Web site and the identifying number of the statute. Federal statute can be found on the Internet at:

FEDERAL STATUTE WEB SITE
http://www4.law.cornell.edu/uscode

The Commonwealth of Pennsylvania has not published their statutes on line, however the Pennsylvania Bar Association has links to Web sites that offer selected sections of Pennsylvania law. To look up a statute, go to the Pennsylvania Bar Association Web site and then to LEGAL LINKS.

PENNSYLVANIA BAR WEB SITE
http://pabar.org

Pennsylvania has organized their laws into 77 numbered Titles. The Titles are organized in any one of three ways: "P.S." (Pennsylvania Statutes), "Pa.C.S." (Pennsylvania Consolidated Statutes) or "Pa.C.S.A." (Pennsylvania Consolidated Statutes Annotated. We will identify statutes by their Title and section within the Title such as (40 P.S. 756), or (23 Pa.C.S 1103), or (20 Pa.C.S.A. 3101). In each case, you can look up the statute by going to the Title number, and then to the section within that Title. If you come across a topic that is of importance to you, you may find it both interesting and profitable to read the law as it is actually written.

A Will is Not Enough in Pennsylvania

CONTENTS

**CHAPTER 1: YOUR ESTATE PLAN CHECK-UP *1*
   DETERMINING YOUR NET WORTH *4*
   MINE, ALL MINE *6*
   PENNSYLVANIA'S INTESTATE LAWS *15*
   THE COST OF PROBATE *18*

**CHAPTER 2: IS PROBATE NECESSARY? *25*
   PROPERTY OWNED JOINTLY *26*
   TRANSFERRING REAL PROPERTY *32*
   THE COST OF AVOIDING PROBATE *38*

**CHAPTER 3: HOW TO AVOID PROBATE *41*
   HOW A TRUST IS CREATED *43*
   THE PROS AND CONS OF A TRUST *45*
   TAXES AND YOUR TRUST *53*
   MAYBE PROBATE ISN'T ALL THAT BAD *59*

**CHAPTER 4: YOUR WILL — YOUR WAY *61*
   THINGS A WILL CAN DO *62*
   CAN YOUR WILL BE CHALLENGED? *72*
   STORING YOUR WILL. *75*

**CHAPTER 5: ARRANGING TO PAY BILLS *79*
   WHO IS RESPONSIBLE TO PAY BILLS? *80*
   JOINT DEBTS *82*
   THINGS THAT CAN BE INHERITED DEBT FREE *90*
   AN ESTATE PLAN FOR THE BANKRUPT *92*

**CHAPTER 6: YOUR BUSINESS ESTATE PLAN *99*
   WHAT'S THE BEST TYPE OF BUSINESS OWNERSHIP? . *102*
   COMPANIES THAT LIMIT LIABILITY *106*
   INSURANCE TO PAY DEBTS AND TAXES *114*

CHAPTER 7: CONTINUING TO CARE *119*
    CARING FOR THE MINOR CHILD *120*
    PROVIDING FOR THE STEPCHILD *130*
    CARING FOR THOSE WHO CAN'T *135*
    THE FUTURE OF ESTATE PLANNING *143*

CHAPTER 8: AN ESTATE PLAN FOR YOUR PERSON *151*
    MAKING BURIAL ARRANGEMENTS *153*
    THE PRE-NEED PLAN *157*
    APPOINTING A HEALTH CARE SURROGATE *168*

CHAPTER 9: A HEALTH CARE ESTATE PLAN *173*
    GUARDIANSHIP: A GOOD THING TO AVOID *175*
    A POWER OF ATTORNEY FOR FINANCES *178*
    PROVIDING FOR LONG TERM CARE *184*

CHAPTER 10: A MEDICAID QUALIFYING PLAN *189*
    WHO IS ENTITLED TO MEDICAID? *190*
    WHAT COUNTS AS A RESOURCE? *197*
    THE SPEND DOWN OPTION *201*
    OPTIONS FOR THE SINGLE APPLICANT *204*
    JUST GIVE IT ALL AWAY *206*

CHAPTER 11: PROTECTING THE HOMESTEAD *213*
    THE LIFE ESTATE STRATEGY *218*
    TRANSFERS THAT PROTECT *220*
    THE MEDICAID APPEAL *226*

CHAPTER 12: GUIDING THOSE YOU LOVE *229*
    POINTING THE WAY *230*
    THE QUICK-FIND FOLDER *236*
    WHEN TO UPDATE YOUR ESTATE PLAN *239*

GLOSSARY *249*

INDEX *263*

When You Need A Lawyer

The purpose of this book is to give the reader a basic understanding of Pennsylvania law as it relates to Wills and other methods of Estate Planning. It is not intended as a substitute for legal counsel or any other kind of professional advice. If you have any legal question, you should seek the counsel of an attorney. When looking for an attorney, consider three things: EXPERTISE, COST and PERSONALITY.

EXPERTISE

The Pennsylvania Bar does not have a program to certify that an attorney is specialized in a particular area of law. This being the case, an attorney in Pennsylvania may not represent to the public that he/she is certified by the state as a specialist in any given area of law. Attorneys are allowed to state that they concentrate on certain areas of law or that they limit their practice to an area of law.

The Pennsylvania Bar Association has a Lawyer Referral Service for some of the larger counties. You can call them at (717) 238-6715 for information about whether there is a referral service in your county; or you can visit their Web site for that information.

 THE PENNSYLVANIA BAR ASSOCIATION WEB SITE
http://www.pabar.org

One of the most reliable ways to find an attorney is through personal referral. Ask your friends, family or business acquaintances if they used an attorney for the field of law that you seek and whether they were pleased with the results.

It is important to employ an attorney who is experienced in the area of law you seek. Your friend may have a wonderful Estate Planning attorney, but if you suffered an injury to your body, then you need an attorney who is experienced in Personal Injury.

Before employing an attorney, ask how long he has practiced that in that field of law and what percentage of his practice is devoted to that type of law.

COST

In addition to the attorney's experience, it is important to check what it will cost in attorney's fees. When you call for an appointment ask what the attorney will charge for the initial consultation and the approximate cost for the service you seek. Ask whether there will be additional costs such as filing fees, accounting fees, expert witness fees, etc.

If the least expensive attorney is out of your price range then you can call the Pennsylvania Legal Services at (800) 322-7572 or your local county Bar Association for the telephone number of the Legal Aid office nearest you.

PERSONALITY

Of equal importance to the attorney's experience and legal fees, is your relationship with the attorney. How easy was it to reach the attorney? Did you go through layers of receptionists and legal assistants before being allowed to speak to the attorney? Did the attorney promptly return your call? If you had difficulty reaching the attorney, then you can expect similar problems should you employ that attorney.

Did the attorney treat you with respect? Did the attorney treat you paternally with a "father knows best" attitude or did the attorney treat you as an intelligent person with the ability to understand the options available to you and the ability to make your own decision based on the information provided to you.

Are you able to understand and easily communicate with the attorney? Is he/she speaking to you in plain English or is his/her explanation of the matter so full of legalese to be meaningless to you?

Do you find the attorney's personality to be pleasant or grating? Sometimes people rub each other the wrong way. It is like rubbing a cat the wrong way. Stroking a cat from head to tail is pleasing to the cat, but petting it in the opposite direction, no matter how well intended, causes friction. If the lawyer makes you feel annoyed or uncomfortable, then find another attorney.

It is worth the effort to take the time to interview as many attorneys as it takes to find one with the right expertise, fee schedule and personality for you.

The Organization of the Book

Many people who have a Will think they have their affairs in order, reasoning that should they die everything will go to the people named in the Will and somehow things will all be taken care of. But this is a simplistic view. There are many more things to consider.
1. What exactly will your beneficiaries inherit?
2. How will your property be transferred?
3. Can you (should you) avoid Probate?
4. Can you avoid a challenge to your Will?

The first four chapters of this book deal with these basic issues. Once you read these chapters you will have an understanding of what will happen to your property should you die, regardless of whether you do, or do not, have a Will.

The rest of the book deals with things a Will <u>cannot</u> do:
Chapter 5. Manage your personal debt
Chapter 6. Limit your business debt
Chapter 7. Provide care for a minor or disabled child
Chapter 8. Appoint someone to make your health care decisions should you be unable to do so
Chapter 9. Appoint someone to handle your finances should you be unable to do so
Chapter 10. Help you qualify for MEDICAID should the need arise
Chapter 11. Protect your home should you need to apply for MEDICAID
Chapter 12. Help your family settle your Estate.

A Will can't do these things but you will be able to do so once you read these chapters and understand what options are available to you under Pennsylvania law.

GLOSSARY

This book is designed for the average reader. Legal terminology has been kept to a minimum. There is a glossary at the end of the book in case you come across a legal term that is not familiar to you.

FICTITIOUS NAMES AND EVENTS

The examples in this book are based loosely on actual events; however, all names are fictitious; and the events, as portrayed, are fictitious.

MALE GENDER USED

Rather than use he/she or himself/herself, for simplicity, we have used the male gender.

Your Estate Plan Check Up 1

To understand why *A Will is Not Enough* you need to know what a Will can and cannot do. One thing a Will can do is make a gift of all you own (your *Estate*). One of the things a Will cannot do is preserve and protect your property during your lifetime. For that, you need to think about risks to your property (poor investments, theft, loss through acts of nature, etc.) and what you can do to minimize or eliminate such risk. In other words, you need an *Estate Plan* for the care and management of your property during your lifetime.

The average person may protest "I don't have an Estate; none the less an Estate Plan." But you do. Everyone who has property, has an Estate Plan. You may never have verbalized your Estate Plan, or even thought about it, but it's there none-the-less. For example, take the case of the college student purchasing his first car. If his parents bankroll the purchase, the son may offer to hold the car jointly with them. The son's Estate is his car. His Estate Plan is to hold the car jointly with his parents so that they will own the car should anything happen to him.

This may not be the best Estate Plan. Holding the car jointly with his parents may make them liable for injuries or damages should the car be involved in an accident. If the young man's parents are familiar with Pennsylvania law, they would be wise to refuse the offer and reassure their son "You can make a Will and make us the beneficiary of your car. But even if you die without a Will, we are your heirs under Pennsylvania law. Either way we will inherit the car. Just make sure to drive carefully and carry enough car insurance."

This is a better Estate Plan. It gives the young man maximum control over his Estate (i.e., his car) during his lifetime. He can sell the car, mortgage it, or trash it, all as he sees fit. If he follows his parent's advice, of driving carefully and purchasing sufficient insurance, his Estate will have maximum protection. If he dies **intestate** (without a Will) and is single and without children, then under Pennsylvania's LAWS OF INTESTATE SUCCESSION, his parents will inherit his Estate. And that is just the way the son wants things at this stage of his life.

Simple situation, simple Estate Plan. But, for most of us, life isn't all that simple. We may own many items of value and have loved ones who rely on us. At some point in our lives, we need to ask:

How can I make sure that my property will be inherited by my choice of beneficiary?

How can I arrange to have my property inherited quickly and at minimum cost?

How can I achieve these goals and yet have maximum control and protection of my property during my lifetime?

We will explore the different ways to answer these questions so that you can decide on an Estate Plan that is best for you. But before doing so you need to know what property you own; i.e., how much your Estate is worth. If you are married and your spouse handles all of the finances, it may be that you have no idea of the value of your Estate.

That was the case with Kristin. She met Matt when they were both at the pinnacle of their careers, but they had no more insight into their precarious position than fireworks in a summer sky just before self-destruct.

Kristin was a model. Not the best, nor the most beautiful, but she made a comfortable living. She moved in a circle of famous models. She reflected off of their radiance, making her appear more attractive than she actually was.

Matt worked in middle management for one of those high tech companies. Like Kristin, he was not particularly gifted but he happened to be in Silicon Valley just at the time the high stakes investors were showing extraordinary, if not misguided, confidence in the industry. The good times were rolling. It never crossed Matt's mind that this would one day end. He spent the money as fast as it came in.

Kristin was impressed with the lavish gifts Matt gave to her. She, and her family, thought she made quite a catch when she announced her engagement. After the wedding she continued to model, but it took a lot of traveling and Matt resented her time away. Eventually, she agreed to stop working altogether. After all, why should she, the wife of a wealthy man, need to continue with the rigors of a model's life of diet and exercise?

Matt never told Kristin about his financial difficulties. All she knew is that he was drinking quite a bit. Her suspicion that he also was into drugs was verified when he died, suddenly, because of an overdose. Her shock and sadness turned to anger when she discovered that all he owned was mortgaged and he was heavily in debt. He even borrowed money from her family without her knowledge!

Matt's creditors took it all. The house, the boat, the Porsche, everything. If only Kristin had investigated the true state of their finances, she could have arranged to set aside the money she earned prior to her marriage and not end up as she did, a destitute widow, past her prime.

DETERMINING YOUR NET WORTH

Even if you are single you may not know the value of your Estate because you have not taken the time to actually sit down and figure it out. To get maximum benefit from this book, you need to take a few minutes to determine your *Net Worth* i.e. the current value of your Estate.

ASSETS:

$_____ Cash (certificates of deposit, bank accounts, etc.)
$_____ Tangible personal property (jewelry, motor vehicles, private art, stamp or coin collections, etc.)
$_____ Cash value of insurance policies
$_____ Securities (stocks, bonds, etc.)
$_____ Cash value of pension plans, IRAs, etc.
$_____ Cash value of a partnership or other business interest
$_____ Real property (residence, time share, lot, condo, cooperatives, etc.)
$_____ TOTAL VALUE OF ASSETS

It may be that you have a loan on your car or home, or any of the above items. You need to subtract away monies you owe to get the bottom line value of what you own:

LIABILITIES

$_____ Private loans
$_____ Mortgage Balance
$_____ Credit card debt
$_____ Car loan or car lease balance
$_____ TOTAL LIABILITIES

A simple subtraction gives you the value of your Estate.
ASSETS — LIABILITIES = NET WORTH

If you are married and hold all property jointly with your spouse, divide by 2 to get the value of your own Net Worth.

A Will is Not Enough in Pennsylvania

Your Net Worth is the value of all that you own, and that is how much your beneficiaries can inherit. Who will inherit your property depends on how your property is *titled* (held or owned).

There are three basic ways to title property:
- ⇨ in *your name only* - or -
- ⇨ *jointly* with another - or -
- ⇨ holding property *in trust for* another.

The way your property is titled determines who will inherit that property:

> Property held in your **name only** will be inherited by the beneficiaries named in your Will.
> If you have no Will, the property will go to your heirs according to Pennsylvania's Laws of Intestate Succession.
>
> Property you hold **jointly** will go to the surviving joint owner(s) of that property.
>
> Property held in **Trust** will go to those you name as the beneficiary of the Trust.
>
> **NOTE** ⇨ If you are married, your spouse may have rights in your property, regardless of the way your property is titled.

We will examine each of these types of ownership in detail so that you can give yourself an Estate Planning check-up, i.e., you can check whether the way you are currently holding your property accomplishes your Estate Planning goals.

MINE, ALL MINE

There's much to be said about holding property in your name only and not jointly or in trust for another. There's maximum control. You can sell it, trade it, mortgage it, with no one to account to, or ask "may I?" How you protect your assets depends on how much security you require. Again, it's all up to you.

As discussed, there are three things to consider when setting up an Estate Plan:

- CONTROL — How to control and protect your Estate during your lifetime.
- BENEFICIARY — How to be sure your Estate goes to the beneficiary of your choice.
- COST — How to transfer your Estate to your beneficiaries at lowest cost.

Holding all of your property in your name only should give you maximum control and protection; but such an Estate Plan may present problems with the cost of transferring your property upon your death. More than likely it will take some sort of Court procedure to transfer that property once you die. The name of the court procedure is **Probate**. In Pennsylvania, the office of the **Register of Wills** handles Probate matters. The Register of Wills is located in the **Orphans' Court**. The Orphans' Court is usually a division of the county Court of Common Pleas. We will refer to property that is transferred to your beneficiary by means of a Probate procedure as your **Probate Estate** (42 Pa.C.S.A. 931, 42 Pa.C.S.A. 951).

Probate can be expensive, so if you keep all of your property in your name only there could be a significant cost to transfer your property to the beneficiaries of your Estate.

Holding property in your name should not create a problem with having your choice of beneficiary inherit your Estate, provided you have a valid Will. But if you die without a Will the Orphans' Court will use the Laws of Intestate Succession to determine who gets your property. Of course it could be that the beneficiaries of your Estate under the Laws of Intestate Succession are exactly who you would have wanted, had you taken the time to prepare a Will. To help you determine if this is the case, we will take a few pages to explain the Law. Those who have a Will might want to skip over the section, however, this information is good to know in the event someone in your family dies without a Will. Once you read the section you will know whether you have a right to inherit their property.

THE FAMILY'S RIGHT TO INHERIT

The Commonwealth of Pennsylvania recognizes the right of the family to inherit property left by the ***decedent*** (the person who died); so the Laws of Intestate Succession cover all possible relationships beginning with the surviving spouse. In order for the spouse to inherit property under the Laws of Intestate Succession, the state of Pennsylvania needs to recognize the union as a valid marriage.

Who Is Your Spouse?

In this era of people challenging the concept of the family unit, those of a philosophical bent may ponder the meaning of marriage. Is it a union of two people in the eyes of God? Is it even a union? Maybe it is just a contract between two people. The Commonwealth of Pennsylvania does not concern itself with such things. If a person dies without a Will, then the state will distribute the property according to the laws of Pennsylvania; and the laws of Pennsylvania determine whether two people are married.

BEING MARRIED IN PENNSYLVANIA

The Commonwealth of Pennsylvania defines a marriage to be a "civil contract by which one man and one woman take each other for husband and wife." The marriage may be established by a formal religious or civil ceremony performed after the couple obtain a licence to marry from the Clerk of the Orphans' Court (23 Pa.C.S. 1102, 23 Pa.C.S. 1301).

Pennsylvania law specifically prohibits the Clerk from issuing a license to people who are:

☒ UNDERAGE

No one under 16 may marry unless the Court grants them permission to do so. Parental consent is required for those over 16 and not yet 18.

☒ INCOMPETENT

Pennsylvania statute prohibits the issuance of a license if either party is "weak minded, insane, of unsound mind . . unless the Court decides it is for the best interest of the applicant and the general public. . ." (23 Pa.C.S. 1304).

☒ FIRST COUSINS OR CLOSER

No license can be issued to those who are parent and child, grandparent and child, siblings, aunt and nephew or uncle and niece, or first cousins. However, under Pennsylvania law, if a married couple are so related, should one of them die, no one may inquire as to the lawfulness of the marriage; i.e., the surviving spouse cannot be convicted of an incestuous relationship with the decedent (23 Pa.C.S. 1703).

☒   CURRENTLY MARRIED

Bigamy is against the law in Pennsylvania, however, if the couple entered their marriage in good faith believing that a prior marriage was ended by divorce or death, then once the prior marriage is properly ended, the couple are considered to be validly married as of the date the prior marriage was ended (23 Pa.C.S. 1702).

☒   SAME SEX MARRIAGE

Vermont is the first state to recognize a same sex marriage, which they refer to as a "civil union." Several other states, including Pennsylvania have passed statutes, specifically denying marital status to couples of the same gender.

THE COMMON LAW MARRIAGE

A Common Law marriage is one that has not been solemnized by ceremony. Pennsylvania Courts have ruled that a Common Law marriage is valid in the state of Pennsylvania, provided the man and woman are each 18 or older (23 Pa.C.S. 3304), and

⇨   they use words (either written or oral) in the present tense, contracting the relationship; for example, saying "I take you as my spouse" - OR -

⇨   the couple live together as man and wife, and then publicly hold themselves out as being married; i.e., tell friends and family that they are married.

The Court cases stating that a Common Law marriage is valid when contracted in this manner, are identified in Pennsylvania statute (23 Pa.C.S. 1103).

Now that you know whether the Commonwealth of Pennsylvania considers you to be married, the next question is whether the state recognizes anyone as your descendant.

Who Is Your Child?

Medical technology has made important contributions to solving the problem of infertility. There are all sorts of solutions, from hormone therapy, to sperm banks that provide donations anonymously, to frozen sperm and/or ova to be thawed and used at a later date, to women who become a surrogate or gestational mother. Solving a set of medical problems has opened the door to a new set of legal problems.

Used to be, the only question was "Who's the father?" Now it could well be "Who's the mother?

Many states have passed legislation to answer these questions. As of the date we went to print, no laws have been passed in the Commonwealth addressing issues relating to assisted conception. That being the case, a child born of such procedure has the same right to inherit as a child conceived the old fashioned way.

THE CHILD BORN OF ARTIFICIAL INSEMINATION

It is presumed the husband of a woman who used artificial insemination to conceive a child, consented to the procedure. If that is not the case, and he is not the father of the child, he can *petition* (ask) the Court to terminate his parental rights and responsibilities. If the husband is successful, the child will not be able to inherit from the husband, nor from his family.

FROZEN SPERM AND THE AFTERBORN CHILD

Under Pennsylvania law a child conceived prior to death and born to the surviving spouse after the death, has the same right to inherit as any other natural child of the decedent (20 Pa.C.S. 2104).

But suppose the child was conceived after death? That question is becoming more of an issue as couples are freezing sperm, ovum or pre-embryo (fertilized cell) for use at a later date. Often the purpose of the procedure is to protect the cell from damage during cancer treatments. If the treatment is unsuccessful, the surviving parent may decide to go ahead with the pregnancy using the frozen reproductive cell. This raises issues of whether the surviving parent has the right to do that without the written consent of the deceased donor; and whether a child born of such procedure is entitled to inherit from the deceased donor.

This inheritance issue has important consequences, not only on the state level but on the federal level as well. A minor child who has lost a parent is entitled to Social Security benefits, but those benefits are based on the state's Laws of Intestate Succession. Section 216 of the Social Security Act provides "a child's insurance benefits can be paid to a child who could inherit under the State's intestate laws." Specifically, a child cannot receive Social Security benefits, unless the child is entitled to inherit under the state's Laws of Intestate Succession.

This issue was brought before the Superior Court in New Jersey. The Court ruled that a child conceived and born after the death of a parent can inherit under New Jersey's Laws of Intestate Succession (*In Re Estate of Kolacy*, 322 N.J.Super. 593 (2000)). Other states have passed laws on this issue. For example, in Virginia the child may not inherit from the deceased donor, unless prior to death the decedent agreed, in writing, to the implantation.

As yet, this question has not been raised in Pennsylvania. But if you decided be a donor, it is important that you express, in writing, whether you want your reproductive cell to be used after your death. You may also want to state whether you intend that a child born of the cell be entitled to inherit your Estate. For those who are married, it is important that your spouse join in the writing; i.e., that you have a written agreement as to the disposition of the reproductive cells in the event of divorce or the death of either party.

Still another legal issue raised because of modern technology is the question of the rights of the Surrogate mother as opposed to the rights of the biological parent who contracted with the Surrogate to bear his/her child.

THE SURROGATE PARENTING CONTRACT

A Surrogate Parenting Contract is an agreement, usually between a married couple and a woman, in which the woman agrees to be the birth mother of a child conceived with the sperm of the husband, or the egg cell of the wife, or the embryo of the married couple. This means that the husband or wife (or both) are the biological parents of the child born of the Surrogate mother.

Some states such as New York and Michigan consider Surrogate Parent Contracts as being against public policy. Other states, such as Florida and Virginia allow a couple to contract with a woman to have their baby, provided the parties conform to the law of the state relating to such contracts. Currently, there are no Pennsylvania laws relating to a Surrogate Parenting Contract. A child born to a Surrogate mother in Pennsylvania has the same rights as any other child born to the mother. If the mother is married, and her husband agreed to the procedure, then he is the legal father of the child.

After the birth the Surrogate parents can agree to the adoption of the child by the intended (biological) parents. Adoption is necessary, regardless of whether either (or both) of the intended parents happen to be the genetic parent of the child. If the child is later adopted, the child will have the same status as any other adopted child.

THE ADOPTED CHILD

An adopted child has the same rights to inherit property from his adoptive parents as does a natural child, provided the child was adopted prior to the age of 18, or had a parent-child relationship with his adopted parents while the child was a minor.

The adopted child has no right to inherit from his natural parents, however if a relative continues to have a family relationship with the child, then that child has the right to inherit from that relative under the Laws of Intestate Succession. Another exception is that of a natural parent who is married to the adoptive parent. For example, if a child loses a parent and is later adopted by a step-parent, the child has the right to inherit from his natural parents and from his adoptive parent as well.

Someone who is adopted after the age of 18, and who did not have a parent-child relationship prior to that time, is not considered a child for the purpose of inheriting property from any member of the family other than his adoptive parents. For example, if the decedent was the adoptive grandparent of someone adopted after the age of 18, unless the grandparent left a gift for that adopted person in his Will, the adopted person has no right to inherit anything from the adoptive grandparent in the Commonwealth of Pennsylvania (20 Pa.C.S.A. 6114 (4)).

THE NON-MARITAL CHILD

A child born out of wedlock has the same rights to inherit from his/her natural father as does one born in wedlock, provided:

- ☑ the decedent acknowledged the child as his own and received the child into his home   - or -

- ☑ the decedent acknowledged the child as his own, and provided support for the child   - or -

- ☑ the decedent married the child's mother - or -

- ☑ paternity was established by clear and convincing evidence, which may include a court determination of paternity (20 Pa.C.S.A. 2107).

Pennsylvania's Laws of Intestate Succession are based on the right of family members to inherit property from the decedent. Now that we know who the Commonwealth of Pennsylvania considers to be your spouse and child, we can examine how much of your Estate they are entitled to inherit.

PENNSYLVANIA'S INTESTATE LAWS

Should you die with property titled in your name only, and without a Will, then the Commonwealth of Pennsylvania provides one for you in the form of the Laws of Intestate Succession. Once your debts, funeral expenses, and the cost of the Probate procedure is paid, whatever is left (your net Probate Estate) is distributed as follows:

❖ MARRIED, NO DESCENDANT, NO PARENT

If you are married with no surviving *descendant* (child, grandchild, great-grandchild, etc.), and no surviving parent, then your net Probate Estate goes to your surviving spouse (20 P.S. 2102(1)).

❖ MARRIED, NO DESCENDANT BUT A SURVIVING PARENT

If at the time of death the decedent was married and had no surviving issue, but he does have a surviving parent, then the spouse gets the first $30,000, and half of whatever is left. The surviving parent(s) get the other half (20 P.S. 2102 (2)).

❖ MARRIED, WITH DESCENDANT

If you are married, with a descendant who is also a descendant of your spouse, your spouse gets the first $30,000 and half of what is ever left. The children get the other half. If you have a descendant, not that of your spouse, your spouse gets half and your descendants get the other half (20 P.S. 2102 (3) and (4)).

❖ SINGLE, WITH CHILDREN

If you are not married but have children, all of whom survive you, then they will share equally in your Probate Estate.

YOUR ESTATE PLAN CHECKUP   *15*

If one or more of your children do not survive you, but your deceased child left surviving descendants, then the descendants inherit the share intended for the deceased child *by representation*. "By representation" is one of those legal terms that is best explained by example:

Suppose a single person has 4 children, Ann, Barry, Carl, David. If he dies without a Will, and all his children survive him, then they each get 25% of his Estate.

CHILD WITHOUT DESCENDANTS DIES BEFORE DECEDENT
If Ann dies before her father leaving no descendants, then Barry, Carl and David divide the Estate between them. Each gets one third of the Probate Estate.

CHILD WITH DESCENDANTS DIES BEFORE DECEDENT
Suppose instead that only Carl and David survived their father. If Ann died leaving 2 children and Barry died leaving one child, then the Estate is divided into 4 shares — one for each surviving child and one share for each deceased child who left a descendant. Carl and David each get their 25% share. Ann's two children share her 25% (they each get 12 1/2%). Barry's child receives the share intended for Barry, namely 25% of the Estate.

✧ SINGLE, NO DESCENDANT
If you leave no spouse or descendant your property is divided equally between your parents. If only one of the decedent's parents is alive, then all of the property goes to that parent. If neither parent is alive, then your Estate is inherited by your siblings, in equal shares by representation. There is no distinction between whole blood and half blood; i.e., a brother of the same set of parents inherits the same as your brother who shares only one parent (20 P.S. 2104(3)).

If you have no brothers, sisters, nephews or nieces, then your Probate Estate is divided in half with half going to your maternal grandparents (or their descendants) and the other half going to your paternal grandparents (or their descendants) (20 P.S. 2103). The order in which the Probate Estate is distributed is fairly complex; so if you have no relatives except at this level, then it is important for you to make a Will, or your property may be inherited by someone you barely know.

THE COMMONWEALTH: HEIR OF LAST RESORT

Property that is either unclaimed or abandoned, goes to the state, so if you die without a Will and you have absolutely no next of kin, then the Commonwealth of Pennsylvania "inherits" your Probate Estate (20 Pa. C.S. 2103 (6)).

 IT ISN'T ALL THAT SIMPLE

The explanation in this book of the Laws of Intestate Succession is abridged. Even though you may now know more about Pennsylvania's Laws of Intestate Succession than you ever wanted to know, there is much more to the law. For example, Pennsylvania law requires that anyone who inherits property according to the Laws of Intestate Succession must survive the decedent by at least 120 hours (5 days). If a relative does not survive by at least 5 days, then that share is distributed as if the person died before the decedent. This rule is not applied if to do so would result in the Commonwealth of Pennsylvania inheriting the property (20 Pa.C.S. 2104).

THE COST OF PROBATE

Holding property in your name only gives you maximum control and protection during your lifetime. If you do not like the way your property will be distributed should you die without a Will, then you can control who inherits your property by preparing a Will. But there is still the question of what it will cost to transfer your Estate to your beneficiaries. In all probability, a Probate procedure will be necessary. How much of your Estate will need to be spent to Probate your Estate?

THE SMALL ESTATE PETITION

There is no need to be concerned about the cost of Probate, if you have **personal property** (bank accounts, securities, etc.) in your name only, worth $25,000 or less. The beneficiary of your Probate Estate can get possession of the property filing a Petition (a request) with the Clerk of the Probate Court asking the judge to issue an order that will enable the beneficiary to get possession of your personal property. The judge will want to know that all of the decedent's bills have been paid, and that the person making the request is entitled to the property. Once he is satisfied that such is the case, he will issue the order (20 Pa.C.S.A. 3102).

The only problem with the Small Probate Petition is that there is no statutory form of the Petition. Unless your beneficiary has some legal background, he will need to employ an attorney to prepare and file the Petition. But the cost of this legal assistance should not be significant.

OTHER NON-PROBATE TRANSFERS

IN ADDITION, to the $25,000, Pennsylvania law allows some things to be transferred to your immediate family in the following order of priority:
- 1st spouse   2nd child
- 3rd parent   4th brother or sister

❖ BANK ACCOUNT UP TO $3,500 ❖

The family member with priority can take possession of any bank account in your name provided the account is worth no more than $3,500 and the bank is given proof that satisfactory funeral arrangements have been made. The proof can be in the form of a funeral bill marked "Paid In Full" or it can be an *Affidavit* (a written statement, sworn to before a Notary Public) signed by the funeral director stating that satisfactory arrangements have been made to pay for the funeral (20 Pa.C.S.A. 3101 (b)).

❖ WAGES OR EMPLOYEE BENEFITS UP TO $5,000 ❖

An employer of a deceased resident of the Commonwealth of Pennsylvania may pay his final wages, salary or any benefit that was due to the decedent (vacation pay, accumulated sick leave pay, etc.) up to $5,000, directly to an immediate family member (20 Pa.C.S.A. 3101 (a)).

❖ PATIENT CARE ACCOUNT UP TO $4,000 ❖

People who are in a facility and receiving medical assistance from the Department of Public Welfare are entitled to a Patient Care Account. The facility can use up to $3,500 of the account to pay for the decedent's funeral. If there is any money left in the account after the funeral director is paid, then the facility can give that money to the immediate family member. The maximum amount that can be paid from a patient care account is $4,000, including the money paid to the funeral home (20 Pa.C.S.A. 3101 (c)).

✧ INSURANCE UP TO $11,000 PAYABLE TO DECEDENT ✧

An insurance policy (life, accident, health) or any annuity or endowment contract that is payable to the decedent or his Estate, can be paid to an immediate family member, provided the amount payable is no more than $11,000. The person appointed by the Court to settle the Estate has the right to take possession of these funds; so if there is going to be a full Probate procedure, the family may decide to have the person appointed by the Court attend to the business of collecting these monies.

The insurance company may not distribute the monies until 60 days after the date of death and provided the Personal Representative has not claimed the funds. The insurance company is protected from any liability for giving the money to the wrong person, provided they get an Affidavit from whomever is requesting the funds verifying that the person making the request has priority (20 Pa.C.S.A. 3101 (d)).

FAMILY MEMBERS NEED TO COOPERATE

You may be wondering what happens if someone takes any of these direct payments "out of turn" or perhaps there is more than one child and that child refuses to share the funds. Pennsylvania statute (20 Pa.C.S.A. 3101) states that anyone who takes the money is answerable to anyone who is harmed by an improper payment.

But this may be small consolation to a wronged sibling. Who wants to sue a brother or sister?

TRANSFERRING THE MOTOR VEHICLE

Your car is another item that can be transferred without a Probate procedure. If the car is held jointly with rights of survivorship, or together with your spouse, then the surviving owner can contact his local Driver and Vehicle Services to change title to his/her name only.

If you own a motor vehicle in your name only, then it is relatively simple for your beneficiary to have title changed to his name. The Department of Transportation (also known as PENNDOT) has different forms that must be completed in order to transfer the motor vehicle. The forms and procedures depend on whether the decedent had a valid Will and who is entitled to inherit the property.

The Bureau of Motor Vehicles publishes a pamphlet:
 VEHICLE TRANSFER AFTER DEATH OF OWNER (Pub. 174)
that explains all of the different procedures and when it is appropriate to use the procedure.

Your beneficiary can get the pamphlet by writing to:
 COMMONWEALTH OF PENNSYLVANIA
 DEPARTMENT OF TRANSPORTATION
 BUREAU OF MOTOR VEHICLES
 HARRISBURG, PA 17104-2516

or by calling (800) 932-4600. If you are calling from out of state, call (717) 391-6190.

THE FULL PROBATE PROCEDURE

Things are not so simple if you own personal property, in your name only, in excess of $25,000 or real property regardless of its value. There will need to be a Probate procedure to transfer the property to the proper beneficiary. The root of the word Probate is "to prove." It refers to the first job of the Orphan's Court, that is, to examine proof of whether the decedent left a valid Will.

The Court's second job is to appoint someone to settle your Estate. If you named someone in your Will to be the **Executor** of your Estate, then the court will appoint that person for the job and issue **Letters Testamentary**, a document giving the Executor authority to administer the Estate. If there is no valid Will, the Court will appoint someone to be the **Administrator** of the Estate and will issue **Letters of Administration.** Both the Executor and the Administrator serve the same function, so for simplicity we will refer to the person appointed by the Court to settle Estate as the **Personal Representative** and the document authorizing him to act, as **Letters.**

The Supreme Court of Pennsylvania has approved basic Probate forms that need to be submitted to the Register of Wills. These forms are printed in the Pennsylvania statutes and entitled ORPHANS' COURT FORMS (RULE 10. REGISTER OF WILLS). The local Orphans' Court Division may have additional forms that need to be completed and filed. Most offices of the Register of Wills have information packages that they can give to your beneficiary.

Those who know their way around the court house, may be tempted to try to fill out the Orphans' Court forms and complete the Probate procedure on their own.

The full Probate procedure is both time consuming and complex. For example, the Personal Representative must publish notice of his appointment in a paper of general circulation and also in a local legal periodical, telling creditors to present their claims for monies owed. He needs to take an inventory of the Probate Estate and where necessary employ an appraiser to evaluate the property. Before he closes the Estate he may need to account for monies spent during the Probate procedure (20 P.a.C.S.A. 3162, 20 P.a.C.S.A. 3301, 20 P.a.C.S.A. 3501.1).

Although the Register's Office will provide information packets, it is not their job to provide the Personal Representative with legal advice. If the Personal Representative makes a mistake, he may be responsible to pay for that mistake. For example, creditors have up to a year from the date of death to present their claims. If the Personal Representative transfers property to the beneficiaries before the year is up, a creditor may come forward and demand payment. The Personal Representative may find himself personally responsible to pay for that debt (20 Pa.C.S. 3385, 20 P.a.C.S.A. 3532).

For most people, it is neither cost effective nor practical to attempt a "do it yourself Probate." Better to employ an attorney to guide them through the procedure. Why risk personal liability when the attorney fees are a proper charge to the Probate Estate?

Compensation for the Personal Representative is also a proper charge to the Probate Estate. The Court must approve fees paid to the Personal Representative and his attorney. Compensation is usually based on the value of the Probate Estate, but the Court will also consider extraordinary or unusual services performed such as settling disputed claims against the Estate (20 P.a.C.S.A. 3537).

THE COST OF A FULL PROBATE PROCEDURE

The Personal Representative and attorney's fees are significant charges to the Probate Estate. Court's have determined that it is reasonable to award $5,000 for the Personal Representative and $5,750 for his attorney, for an Estate of $100,000 (*Johnson Estate*, 4 Fid.Rep.2d 6, 8 (O.C.Del.Co. 1983)) and that was back in 1983!

In addition, some or all of the following may be charged to your Probate Estate:
- $$ Court fees to file the Probate procedure
- $$ The cost of a bond that the Court may order for the protection of your Probate Estate
- $$ The cost of notifying your creditors which may include publishing notice, and mailing notice to them by registered or certified mail
- $$ The cost of an appraisal of Estate property
- $$ Accounting fees to file the proper tax returns, prepare the inventory, and account for monies spent during the Probate procedure
- $$ The cost of transferring property to the proper beneficiary; i.e., recording fees, broker fees to sell securities or real estate

You may be thinking that Probate is a good thing to avoid. Why should your Personal Representative go through all that effort to settle your Estate? Why should your beneficiaries wait a year or more, and pay all these fees to inherit your Estate?

There are different ways to arrange your Estate so that your beneficiaries can immediately inherit your Estate without incurring unnecessary costs. In the next two chapters we will examine each of these methods in detail.

Is Probate Necessary? 2

Many people think that only wealthy people need to make plans to avoid Probate, yet each year, heirs of relatively modest estates, spend thousands of dollars to settle an Estate. A bit of Estate Planning could have eliminated most, if not all, of the cost (and hassle) suffered by those families.

If you have a small Estate and only one or two beneficiaries, then it is not all that difficult to arrange your finances to eliminate the need for Probate altogether. All you need do is title your property so that it automatically goes to your beneficiaries. There are many ways to arrange your finances to get this result. The most common method is to hold property jointly with another. Such an arrangement is the Estate Plan of choice for most married couples. Husband and wife often hold all of their property jointly, so that the surviving spouse has complete and immediate access to their property without any need for Probate.

Holding property jointly may not be the most desirable method for the single person, or for the surviving spouse who is now single. There are other ways to ensure that your property is inherited quickly and without cost to your heirs. In this chapter we explore the pros and cons of different methods of holding property so that it can be transferred without the need for Probate.

PROPERTY OWNED JOINTLY

Bank accounts, securities, motor vehicles, real property can all be owned by two or more people. If one of the owners dies, then the survivor(s) continue to own their share of the property. Who owns the share belonging to the decedent depends on Pennsylvania law and how ownership of the property was set up.

THE JOINT BANK ACCOUNT

When a bank account is opened in two or more names, the owners of the account sign an agreement with the bank stating who is to have access to the account during the lifetime of the account owners; i.e. whether each owner has full authority to make a withdrawal, or whether two signatures are required. The agreement should also say how the ownership of the account is to be transferred should one of the owners die. Unless the agreement with the bank states differently, it is presumed that there are **rights of survivorship** meaning that the share belonged to the deceased joint owner now belongs to the surviving joint owners (7 Pa.C.S. 604).

The benefit of a joint account is that whatever remains in the account goes directly to the suriviving joint owners of the account without the need to go through a Probate procedure to get that money. Many married couples own a joint banking account for just that reason.

A parent whose only asset is a bank account might decide that a simple way to avoid Probate is to make his child joint owner of the account. But there are potential problems associated with holding an account jointly with a child.

⊠ OVERREACHING

Making your child a joint owner of the account gives the child free access to the account. Monies may be withdrawn without your knowledge or authorization. You may be thinking that couldn't happen because you would immediately know of the withdrawal, and you could force the child to return the money. That may be true when you are healthy and alert. But in this ever aging society, it is likely that you will live to an advanced age and not be as aware as you are today. And if you have two children and decided to hold your account jointly with them, then there may be a problem with how the funds are distributed should you die.

That was the case with Amanda. All she had when her husband died, was a bank account worth $50,000. She wanted to be sure that the money would go to her two sons, Robert and Leon without the need for Probate. She went to the bank with her two sons and opened a new survivorship account with all three names on the account as joint owners.

Several years passed without incident. As Amanda aged, her health began to fail, and she became more and more dependent on Robert. She needed his assistance to take her to the doctor, to do her shopping, and of course take care of her finances. Robert had a wife and two children, so it was hard for him to care for his family and his mother as well. Leon was single, yet he never seemed to have the time to help care for his mother. And Robert resented that.

Finally, Amanda died.

After the funeral, Leon asked Robert about the bank account "Didn't Mom have a joint account in our names?"

"Yeah, but I closed it out. There was only a few thousand left, and I used it for her funeral."

Leon thought it strange that all of the money was gone, so he went to the bank and asked to see the record of withdrawals. He found that over the last two years Robert had written several large checks to himself. There was only $7,000 left in the account when Robert closed it out, within a week of her death.

Leon fumed for several weeks before he brought up the subject. Robert's face flushed when Leon asked about the money. Leon did not know if it was from anger or embarrassment. He soon learned that it was both when Robert asked "Where were you for the past two years? You never once helped. Did you know she became incontinent at the end? Who cleaned up? Not you. She blessed me every day. She often said she would have been dead long ago if it wasn't for me. She wanted me to have that money!"

"Mom never said anything to me about wanting you to have the money. She never asked for my help and neither did you. It isn't right for you to throw this up to me now."

The boys never spoke of the money again. But then there were few times that they ever spoke to each other after that.

Overreaching isn't the only problem with a joint account, there is also the problem of liability.

☒ POTENTIAL LIABILITY

If you hold a bank account jointly with your adult child and that child is sued or gets a divorce, then the child may need to disclose his ownership of the joint account. In such a case, you may find yourself spending money to prove that the account was established for convenience only and that all of the money in that account really belongs to you.

Because of these inherent problems, you might want to hold the funds so that your beneficiary does not gain access to the monies until and unless you die. You can do so by holding your account in beneficiary form.

THE BENEFICIARY ACCOUNT

As explained, the terms of a bank account are established when a bank account is opened. Your agreement gives directions about who can access your account during your lifetime, but it can also give directions about what to do with the account should you die. If you hold the account in your name only and do not give any such directions, then should you die while the account is open, the monies in your account will become part of your Probate Estate and will be distributed in the same way as any other item that you hold in your name only.

One way to avoid Probate of the account, yet retain full control of the account during your lifetime, is to name one or more persons to be the beneficiary of your account.

There are two forms of beneficiary account. Your contract with the bank can direct the bank to hold your account *in trust for* ("ITF") one or more beneficiaries that you name; or you can have a contract with the bank that directs the bank to *Pay On Death* ("POD"), all of the money in the account, to one or more beneficiaries that you name. Under Pennsylvania law, unless your contract with the bank says differently:

⇨ The beneficiary does not have access to the account during your lifetime.

⇨ You, as the owner of the account, have complete control over the account. You can add to it or close it or change beneficiaries without asking anyone's permission to do so.

(7 P.S. 605, 20 Pa.C.S.A. 6304).

If you are married, you may want to hold the account jointly with your spouse with directions to the bank to give the funds to one or more beneficiaries that you name. For example, ELDON JONES and LORRAINE JONES, JT TEN
POD ELDON JONES, JR. AND FRED JONES

Unless the contract with the bank says differently:

⇨ During their lifetime, Eldon and Lorraine each own an equal share of the account, unless it is shown that each contributed a different amount.

⇨ The children (Eldon, Jr. and Fred) have no right to the account during the lifetime of their parents.

⇨ If either Eldon or Lorraine dies, then the surviving party owns the account, and is free to close the account or change the beneficiary of the account.

⇨ Once Eldon and Lorraine are deceased, their sons share the money in the account equally. Should one son die before his parent, the remaining son will inherit the entire account.

THE TRANSFER ON DEATH SECURITY

The Pennsylvania law for securities is similar to the statute for banks. You instruct the holder of the security to Pay-On-Death or **TRANSFER ON DEATH ("TOD")** to a named beneficiary once you die.

As with the POD account, you can hold a security jointly with another with instructions that once you both die, the security is to be transferred to a beneficiary.

For example, you can hold a securities account as follows:
MARIO BONO and OLIVIA BONO
as joint tenants with rights of survivorship
TRANSFER ON DEATH TO DOMINICK BONO

When both of his parents die, Dominick will inherit the securities. Should Dominick die before his parents, then the securities will go to the Estate of the last parent to die.

Pennsylvania statute requires that if a security is held jointly for the benefit of another then the owners of the security must own that security as with Rights of Survivorship and not as Tenants In Common. This means that should one of the joint owners die, his share goes to the remaining joint owner. The surviving joint owner then has the option of continuing holding the security for the same beneficiary or leaving it to someone else by changing the name of the beneficiary of the account (20 Pa.C.S.A. 6402, 20 Pa.C.S.A.6407, 20 Pa.C.S.A. 6410).

TRANSFERRING REAL PROPERTY

If you own real property together with another, then who will own the property upon your death depends on how the current owner is identified on the face of the deed. The top paragraph of the deed should identify the person who transferred the property to you, namely "Grantor." The person to whom the property was transferred is called the "Grantee."

The form of the deed might look similar to the following:

> THIS DEED, made this day, March 2, 2003, between ROBERT TRAYNOR, whose address is 123 Main Street, York, PA, Grantor
> and
> ALFRED CODY and ROBERT CODY, JOINT TENANTS WITH RIGHT OF SURVIVORSHIP, Grantee . . .

As the deed states, there is a Right of Survivorship. Should either Alfred or Robert die, the survivor will own the property 100%. Nothing need be done to establish that ownership. The name of the deceased owner remains on the deed, so the surviving owner needs to keep a certified copy of the death certificate to present at closing should the surviving owner decide to sell or mortgage the property.

▤ DEED HELD AS HUSBAND AND WIFE

If you were married at the time you took title to real property and the deed identifies you as being married, for example: TODD AMES AND SUSAN AMES, H/W or
TODD AMES AND SUSAN AMES, HIS WIFE or
TODD AMES AND SUSAN AMES, HUSBAND AND WIFE
then you and your spouse now own the property as *Tenants by the Entirety*.

A Tenancy by Entirety is much the same as a Joint Tenancy with right of survivorship. Should one spouse die, and providing they are married at the time of death, the surviving spouse owns the property 100%.

▤ DEED HELD AS TENANTS IN COMMON

You might have a deed that names you and another person as Grantee, followed by TENANTS IN COMMON. In such case, should you die, your share will go to whoever you named as beneficiary of that share in your Will. If you die without a Will, the Laws of Intestate Succession determine who will inherit your share of the property.

Although it is presumed that joint owners of a bank account have Rights of Survivorship, there is no similar assumption for real property. If a deed names two unmarried people as Grantee and does not say that there is a Right of Survivorship, then they own the property as Tenants-In-Common. For example, there is no right of survivor if property is held as:
Alfred Cody and Robert Cody   - or -
Alfred Cody and Robert Cody, Jointly
Should either owner die, his share will go to his Estate and not to the surviving joint owner (68 P.S. 110).

📄 DEED WITH A LIFE ESTATE

A *Life Estate* interest in real property means that the person who owns the Life Estate has the right to live in that property until he/she dies. You can identify a Life Estate interest by examining the face of the deed. If somewhere on the face of the deed you see the phrase RESERVING A LIFE ESTATE, then the Grantee cannot take possession of the property until the owner of the Life Estate dies. For example, suppose the granting paragraph of the deed reads:

> THIS DEED, made this day, July 1, 2002, between ROSE CAVALLO, a single woman whose address is 5 Olive St. York, PA, Grantor and, SALVATORE CAVALLO, Grantee,
>
> . . .
>
> RESERVING A LIFE ESTATE TO ROSE CAVALLO
>
> . . .

Rose Cavallo (the Grantor) is the owner of the Life Estate. Salvatore Cavallo (the Grantee) is the owner of the *Remainder Interest*. Rose has the right to occupy the premises during her lifetime or to rent it out and receive the income from the property. During Rose's lifetime, Salvatore has no right to the possession of, or the income from, the property. Once Rose dies, Salvatore will own the property and is free to take possession of the property and to lease, sell, or transfer it, as he sees fit.

If you are an owner of the Life Estate interest, upon your death, no Probate procedure will be necessary to transfer the property to the owner of the Remainder Interest.

TRANSFERRING PENNSYLVANIA REAL PROPERTY

No Probate procedure will be necessary if you hold property in Pennsylvania:
- ➪ as the owner of a Life Estate   - or -
- ➪ as Tenant By The Entirety   - or -
- ➪ as a Joint Tenant with Right of Survivor

In each of these cases, upon your death, the surviving owner will own the property 100%. If there is a Probate procedure for other property owned by the deceased Grantee, then a title search at the time of transfer will reveal the fact that the Grantee died. If no Probate is necessary, then all the surviving Grantee need to do is to keep a certified copy of the death certificate, and receipts showing that all applicable Estate and Inheritance Taxes have been paid, to present at closing should the surviving Grantee decide to sell or transfer the property.

WHEN PROBATE IS NECESSARY

If you own Pennsylvania property in your name only, or as a Tenant-In-Common, it will take a Probate procedure to transfer property to your intended beneficiary.

OUT OF STATE PROPERTY

This chapter relates only to property that you own in Pennsylvania. If you own property in another state or country, then the laws of that state or country determine who has the right to inherit property in that state or country. Whether or not there are Rights of Survivorship depend on the laws of that state. Some states are the same as Pennsylvania, requiring that the deed specifically state that there are Rights Of Survivorship. Other states do not require that the deed indicate a Right of Survivor. In those states, property owned as a Joint Tenant means that the surviving owner inherits the property.

If you own out of state property jointly with another, it is important that you check with an attorney in that state to be sure that your share of the property will go to the person of your choice.

In addition to Right of Survivorship, a surviving spouse may have rights in real property owned by a decedent spouse, even though the deed was in the decedent's name only. This is the case in Community property states (Arizona, California, New Mexico, Louisiana, etc.). Other states may have Dower rights or other statutory rights that a surviving spouse has in the property. In the next chapter, we will discuss the statutory rights of a surviving spouse in real property located in the Commonwealth of Pennsylvania. If you are married and own property in your name only in another state, you need to determine the rights of your spouse in that state as well.

Still another concern is whether a Probate procedure will be necessary to transfer out of state property that you own to your beneficiary.

TRANSFERRING OUT OF STATE PROPERTY

Each state is in charge of the way property located in that state is transferred. Most state laws are similar to Pennsylvania, namely, property you hold as a Joint Tenant with Right of Survivorship or property in which you hold a Life Estate interest are transferred without the need for Probate. Property you own as a Tenant In Common or in your name only may require a Probate procedure in order to transfer the property to your beneficiary.

If you own property in your name only in this state and in another state, upon your death it may be necessary to have a Probate procedure in Pennsylvania, and an *ancillary* (secondary) Probate procedure in the state where the property is located. This could have the effect of doubling the cost of Probate.

Still another problem with out of state property is the matter of taxes. Some states have an inheritance or transfer tax. Estate and Inheritance taxes may be due in the state where the property is located as well as here in Pennsylvania. It may be necessary to file a tax return in two states. In addition to increased taxes, this can double the cost of the accounting fees.

If you own property in another state, it is important to consult with an attorney to learn the answers to all of these questions, namely:

Who will inherit my property under the laws of the state where it is located?

Will a Probate procedure be necessary to transfer that property to my beneficiaries?

Will a state inheritance tax need to be paid?

THE COST OF AVOIDING PROBATE

If you find that Probate will be necessary to transfer real property that you own in Pennsylvania or elsewhere, you may decide that the cost of Probate is too expensive. You may be tempted to go for the quick fix of having the deed to the property changed so that you are joint owners with the intended beneficiary of the property; or you may decide to transfer the property to your intended beneficiary and keep a Life Estate for yourself.

This will avoid Probate, but it may not be the best Estate Plan because you will not have maximum control over the property during your lifetime. If you hold real property as a Joint Tenant or as a Life Tenant, you will not be able to sell that property during your lifetime without getting permission from your beneficiary. And if the beneficiary gives permission and the property is sold, the beneficiary will have the legal right to share in the proceeds of the sale.

You may be thinking "I can make my son joint owner of my home and avoid any need for Probate. I trust him to do what I want with the property. If I decide to sell, I know he won't ask for any part of the proceed regardless of his legal right to those funds."

And all that may be true, but it may cost you more in taxes to sell your property than if you kept the property in your name only.

Under today's law, you can sell your home without paying a Capital Gains tax, provided you lived there for 2 of the prior 5 years and the Capital Gains on the sale is not greater than $250,000 ($500,000 if married). If you sell your home after making the Life Estate transfer (or making your child a Joint Tenant), then unless your child occupies the home as his primary residence, his share of the property is subject to a Capital Gains tax.

If your son does not take his share of the proceeds, then why should he pay any Capital Gains tax?

In such case, you'll be the one to pay the tax on your son's share of the proceeds.

Is there a better way to avoid Probate?

Maybe. Read on.

How To Avoid Probate   3

TRUE OR FALSE?
(   ) If you have a Will, then Probate will be necessary.
(   ) Probate will be necessary if you don't have a Will.
(   ) Probate is necessary if you own property that is worth more than $25,000.

If you answered false to all of the above, you are either a lawyer, or you carefully read the last chapter.

All of these sentences are false because all of your property may pass to your beneficiaries automatically, without the need for Probate, such as property held Jointly with Right of Survivor, or in a Pay-On-Death account. The point we were trying to make is:

> Whether a Probate procedure is necessary has nothing to do with whether there is a Will, or even how much money is involved. The determining factor is how the property is titled (owned).

There are three basic ways to title property:
- ❖ in your name only
- ❖ jointly with another
- ❖ in trust for another

Chapter 1 examined the pros and cons of holding property in your name only, with the biggest "con" being that Probate may be necessary.

41

In Chapter 2 we noted that holding property jointly with another solved the Probate problem, but at the sacrifice of the control and protection offered by keeping property in your name only. In this Chapter we examine another option which may be the solution to these problems, namely the ***Revocable Living Trust*** (also known as an ***Inter Vivos Trust***).

A Revocable Living Trust is designed to care for your property during your lifetime and then to distribute your property once you die without the need for Probate. You may have been encouraged to set up such a Trust by your financial planner, attorney, or accountant. Even people of modest means are being encouraged to use a Trust as the basis of their Estate Plan. But Trusts also have their pros and cons. Before getting into that, let's first discuss what a Trust is and how it works.

HOW A TRUST IS CREATED

To create a Revocable Living Trust, an attorney prepares a Trust Agreement in accordance with the client's needs and desires. The "Agreement" refers to the fact that the person setting up the Trust (the *Trustor* or *Settlor*) is contracting with someone to be the *Trustee* (manager) of property placed in the Trust. By signing the Trust Agreement, the Trustee agrees to manage the Trust property according to the directions given in the Trust Agreement. If the Trustor is the one who places property into the Trust, then he is referred to as the *Grantor*. We will refer to the Revocable Living Trust as the "Living Trust" or just the "Trust" and the person setting up the Trust as the "Grantor." Usually the Grantor appoints himself as Trustee so that he is in total control of property that he places into the Trust. In that case he signs the Trust Agreement as the Grantor and also as the Trustee who agrees to follow the terms of the Trust Agreement.

The Trust Agreement also names a *Successor Trustee* who will take over the management of the Trust property should the Trustee resign, become disabled or die.

Once the Trust document is properly signed, the Grantor transfers property into the Trust. The Grantor does this by changing the name on the account from his individual name to his name as Trustee. For example, if Elaine Richards sets up a Trust naming herself as Trustee, and she wishes to place her bank account into the Trust then all she need do is instruct the bank to change the name on the account from ELAINE RICHARDS to:

    ELAINE RICHARDS, TRUSTEE OF THE ELAINE RICHARDS REVOCABLE TRUST AGREEMENT DATED JULY 12, 2002.

When the change is made, all the money in the account becomes Trust property. Elaine (wearing her Trustee hat) has total control of the account, taking money out, and putting money in, as she sees fit. Similarly, if she wants to put real property into the Trust all she need do is have her attorney or a title insurance company prepare and record a new deed with the owner of the property identified as:

    ELAINE RICHARDS, TRUSTEE of the ELAINE RICHARDS REVOCABLE TRUST AGREEMENT DATED JULY 12, 2002.

The Trust document states how the Trust property is to be managed during Elaine's lifetime. Should Elaine become disabled the Trust will provide for her Successor Trustee to take over and manage the Trust property. Because the Trust is revocable, if she wishes, Elaine can terminate the Trust at any time and have the Trust property placed back into her own individual name.

If Elaine does not revoke her Trust during her lifetime, once she dies the Trust becomes irrevocable, and her Successor Trustee must follow the terms of the Trust Agreement as it is written.

If the Trust says to give the Trust property to certain beneficiaries, then the Successor Trustee will do so; and in most cases without any Probate procedure. If the Trust directs the Successor Trustee to continue to hold property in Trust and use the money to take care of a member of Elaine's family, then the Successor Trustee will do so.

THE PROS AND CONS OF A TRUST

A Living Trust has many good features.

☆ AVOID PROBATE

As discussed in Chapter 1, Probate can be time consuming and expensive. Both the Personal Representative and his attorney are entitled to payment for their services. These fees can be significant. It may be necessary to hire accountants and appraisers, as well. If you have property in two states, then two Probate procedures may be necessary (one in each state) and that could have the effect of doubling the cost of Probate. If the Trust is properly drafted and your property placed into the Trust, you should be able to avoid Probate altogether.

☆ AVOID A CHALLENGE TO YOUR ESTATE PLAN

A Trust operates much like a Will because it provides for the distribution of your Estate when you die. Unlike a Will, it is not subject to Probate, so no Court is charged with the duty of "proving" that your Trust is valid. Your Successor Trustee can distribute your property as you direct, without asking anyone's permission to do so, and without giving the Court or any outside party an opportunity to examine the document. This does not mean that your Estate Plan cannot be challenged; but if the Trust is drafted according to the law, and not for the purpose of ripping off your creditors, or cutting off your spouse's right to inherit, it will be very difficult for anyone to challenge the document.

☆ CARE FOR FAMILY MEMBER

You can make provision in your Trust to care for a minor child or family member after you die. If your family member is immature or a born spender, you can set up the Trust to protect the beneficiary from squandering the inheritance. If you are concerned that your beneficiary will spend, within months, what it took you a lifetime to earn, consider having an attorney prepare a Trust that will spread the inheritance over an extended period of time. Your Trust can direct the Trustee to give a certain amount of money every 5 or 10 years; for example you can direct the Trustee to give part of the gift when the beneficiary reaches 25, another amount when he reaches 35, and then 45, etc.

If your intended beneficiary has a creditor problem, you can set up a **Spendthrift Trust**. You can direct your Successor Trustee to use the Trust funds for your beneficiary's health care, education, and living expenses, and nothing else. With a properly drafted Spendthrift Trust provision the Trust funds should be protected from the claims of the creditors of the beneficiary. The only exception is money owed by the beneficiary for alimony or child support. Pennsylvania statute requires that the beneficiary of a Trust who is entitled to receive income from the Trust be responsible to make support payments as ordered by the Court. If the beneficiary has no other source of income, then he will need to use the income from the Trust to make those payments (20 Pa.C.S.A. 6112).

NO CREDITOR PROTECTION FOR GRANTOR

Property you place in your Revocable Living Trust is freely accessible to you. It is likewise accessible to your creditors both before and after your death. Pennsylvania Courts have ruled that the Settlor of a Trust " ... could not create a valid spendthrift trust in her property for her own use as against her creditors, and the property is subject to her debts and contracts as fully as if no spendthrift provision existed." (*Bowers' Trust Estate*, 346 Pa. 85 (1943); 29 A.2d 519).

☆ PRIVACY

Your Trust is a private document. No one but your Successor Trustee and your beneficiaries need ever read it. If you have a Will, once it is admitted to Probate it becomes part of the County records (20 Pa.C.S. 921). Anyone can examine the county records, read your Will and see who you did (or did not) provide for in your Will. Other Probate documents such as the inventory of your Probate Estate, creditor's claims, etc. are also open to public scrutiny. It is not much of a stretch to predict that in the future, Court records will be published on the Internet!

☆☆ AVOID GUARDIANSHIP

Once you have a Trust, you do not need to worry about who will take care of your property should you become disabled or too aged to handle your finances. The person you appointed as Successor Trustee will take over the care of the Trust property if you are unable to do so. If you do not have a Trust, and become incapacitated, a Court may need to appoint a Guardian to care for your property. The cost to establish and maintain the guardianship is charged to you. As we will see in Chapter 9, such legal procedures can be expensive and once established cannot be terminated unless you die or are restored to health (20 Pa.C.S.A. 5511).

With all these perks, you may be ready to call your attorney to make an appointment to set up a Trust, but before doing so there are a few things you need to consider.

THE CONS

☒ COMPLEXITY

A Trust is a fairly complex document, sometimes more than 40 pages long. It needs to be that long because you are establishing a vehicle for taking care of your property during your lifetime, as well as after your death. Your Trust may be written in "legalese," so it may take you considerable time and effort to understand it.

It is important to have your Trust document prepared by an attorney who has the patience to work with you until you fully understand each paragraph of the document and are satisfied that what it states is what you really want.

☒ COST

Because of the thoroughness of the document and the fact that it is custom designed for you, a Trust will cost much more to draft than a simple Will. In addition to the initial cost of the Trust, it can be expensive to maintain the Trust should you become disabled or die. Your Successor Trustee has the right to charge for his duties as Trustee, as well as to charge for any specialized services performed. A financial institution can charge to serve as Successor Trustee, and also charge to manage the Trust portfolio. If you decide to appoint a financial institution to serve Successor Trustee, then it is important that you compare the fee schedules of different institutions.

If you choose a professional (lawyer, accountant, financial planner, etc.) to serve as Trustee, it is important to have a fee agreement stating what will be charged for his duties as Trustee and what will be charged for professional work done on behalf of the Trust. The agreement should be in writing and signed by you and your Successor Trustee. The fee agreement can be included in the Trust document with a provision that whoever accepts the job of Successor Trustee, agrees to accept the fee as provided in the Trust document.

You may decide to appoint your spouse or a family member as Successor Trustee, who may want little, or no, compensation. But regardless of who you choose to be Successor Trustee, you need to come to an agreement as to what will be charged to manage the Trust. If you make no provision for fees in your Trust Agreement, then your Successor Trustee has the right to take a reasonable fee from the Trust property. If the beneficiaries of the Trust do not think the fee is reasonable, they can ask the Court to set the fee (20 Pa.C.S.A. 7185). But that will probably trigger a legal battle. It is better that you set the fee, and. hopefully, head off unnecessary legal expenses.

☒ YOU MAY NEED YOUR SPOUSE'S PERMISSION TO TRANSFER PROPERTY INTO YOUR TRUST

Most married couples prepare a Trust as part of their overall Estate Plan. Sometimes a married person has a Trust that was prepared prior to the marriage, or he may decide to create a Trust to care for children from a previous marriage. In such case, it may be necessary to have the spouse agree, in writing, to transfers into the Trust. The reason permission is needed is the ***Elective Share***. The Grantor's spouse has the right to inherit as much as allowed under Pennsylvania law, unless the spouse signs a waiver giving up that right. The Elective Share is equal to one third of the property owned or controlled by the decedent, including:

⇨ The decedent's Probate Estate

⇨ Property held in the decedent's Living Trust

⇨ Gifts in excess of $3,000 given by the decedent within one year of the date of death; and

⇨ Non-probate transfers such as Pay-On-Death or joint bank accounts, Transfer-On-Death securities, etc.

The proceeds of an insurance policy is not included; nor is any of the decedent's pension that is payable to someone other than the surviving spouse. Pennsylvania statute (20 Pa.C.S.A. 2203) gives a complete list of items that are and are not included when computing the Elective Share.

If you make transfers into your Trust without your spouse's permission, and without providing for the Elective Share, your surviving spouse can go to the Orphan's Court and demand that as much property be transferred from the Trust (or from anyone in possession of your property) as is necessary to make up the Elective Share.

☒ PROBATE MIGHT STILL BE NECESSARY

The Trust only works for those items that you place in the Trust. If you own property as a Tenant-In-Common, when you die, a Probate procedure might be necessary to transfer your share of the property to your beneficiary. If you purchase a security in your name only, without a "Transfer On Death" designation to a beneficiary or to your Trust, then a Probate procedure may be necessary to determine who should inherit the security.

The attorney who prepares the Trust usually creates a safety net for such situations. He prepares a Will for you to sign at the same time you sign the Trust. The Will makes your Trust the beneficiary of your Probate Estate. If you own anything in your name only, should a Probate procedure be necessary, the Will directs your Personal Representative to make that asset part of your Trust by transferring the asset to your Successor Trustee. Your Successor Trustee will add that asset to your Trust (20 Pa.C.S.A. 2515).

The Will prepared by the attorney is called a "Pour Over Will" because it is designed to "pour" any asset titled in your name only, into the Trust. Having the Will ensures that all of your property will go to the beneficiaries named in your Trust. But the downside of holding property in your name only is that a full Probate procedure may be necessary just to get that asset into your Trust. If avoiding Probate is your goal, holding property, in your name only, defeats that goal.

You can ensure that a Probate procedure will not be necessary by transferring your assets into your Trust during your lifetime, but if you neglect to put something into your Trust, the Pour Over Will stands by to transfer that asset into your Trust.

HOW TO AVOID PROBATE *51*

☒ ☆ THE TRUST IS LEGALLY ENFORCEABLE

Any beneficiary of the Trust can petition the Orphan's Court to settle a dispute arising out of the administration of the Trust. For example, if the Trustee is not properly administering the Trust, the beneficiaries can petition the Court to remove the Trustee and appoint another to serve as Successor Trustee (20 Pa.C.S. 7121).

We gave this section a cross and a star, because the right to have a Trust enforced or administered by a court is a double edged sword. It is great to have the Court protect the rights of your beneficiaries, but the cost of a Court battle could be greater than using Probate to transfer your Estate. Worse yet, your beneficiaries are at a disadvantage because the Trustee can charge the legal expenses to your Trust, while the beneficiaries must pay for their legal battles out of their own pocket. Even if the beneficiaries win the argument, the Trustee's legal fees are paid from the Trust, so there is just that much less for the beneficiaries to inherit.

TAXES AND YOUR TRUST

Putting property into a Revocable Living Trust does not shield that property from taxes. All of the property held in a Revocable Living Trust is taxed as if the Grantor were holding that property in his/her own name. If the property earns income, then income taxes will be due, and at the same rate as the Grantor would have paid if he had no Trust. Once the Grantor dies, both the federal and state government have the right to impose an *Estate Tax* on property transferred to a beneficiary as a result of the death. All the property owned as of the date of death becomes the decedent's *Taxable Estate.* This includes real property (homestead, vacant lots, etc.) and personal property (cars, life insurance policies, business interests, securities, IRA accounts, etc.). It includes property held in the decedent's name alone, as well as property that he held jointly or in Trust. It also includes gifts given by the decedent during his lifetime that exceeded $10,000 per person, per year. That *Annual Gift Tax Exclusion* is now based on the cost of living index and in 2002 was increased to $11,000 (IRS 2503(b)).

For most of us, this is not a concern because no federal or Pennsylvania Estate Tax need be paid unless the decedent's Taxable Estate exceeds the federal *Estate Tax Exclusion* amount. That value is currently one million dollars and is scheduled to go even higher:

YEAR	ESTATE TAX EXCLUSION AMOUNT
2003	$1,000,000
2004-2005	$1,500,000
2006-2008	$2,000,000
2009	$3,500,000

In 2010 the federal Estate Tax is scheduled to be phased out altogether; however in 2011, the Estate Tax will be reinstated unless lawmakers change the tax law once again.

A TRUST TO REDUCE ESTATE TAXES

Under current law, Estates of those who die in 2010 are exempt from Federal Estate taxes, but in 2011, the Estate Tax is scheduled to be reinstated and Estates worth more than $1,000,000 will once again be subject to a sizeable Estate Tax. A couple with an Estate in excess of a million dollars can reduce the risk of an Estate Tax by setting up his and her Trusts, so that each person can take advantage of his own Exclusion Amount.

For example, if a couple owns 2 million dollars, they can separate their funds into two Trusts each valued at one million dollars. The Trusts can be set up so that a surviving spouse can use the income from the deceased partner's Trust for living expenses. In this way, their standard of living need not be reduced by separating their funds into two Trusts.

If they do not wish to separate funds, they can set up a single Joint Trust that separates into two Trusts once one partner dies. Again, the surviving spouse is free to use the income from both Trusts. Once both partners are deceased, the beneficiaries of their respective Trusts will inherit the funds, hopefully with no Estate Tax due.

If the couple makes no Trust provision, and they hold their property jointly, then the last to die will own the two million dollars with only one Estate Tax Exclusion available. That means one million dollars is subject to a sizeable Estate Tax.

A Revocable Living Trust is a relatively simple way for a married couple to reduce, if not eliminate, the need to pay Estate taxes; however, there is still the problem of the federal Gift Tax and the Capital Gains Tax.

THE PENNSYLVANIA ESTATE TAX

In addition to the federal Estate Tax there is also the Pennsylvania Estate Tax. The Pennsylvania Estate Tax is based on the federal Estate Tax. The federal government imposes a tax on all property transferred because of the death. The federal government then grants an Estate Tax Exclusion, so that no tax need be paid unless the amount transferred is more than a given value. That Exclusion amount is currently one million dollars. The Pennsylvania Estate tax is called a "pick-up" tax, because the state collects the tax that would have gone to the federal government had it not been for the federal Estate Tax Exclusion. Any money paid by the beneficiary for the Pennsylvania Estate Tax is credited toward taxes that are due for the Pennsylvania Inheritance Tax.

As with the federal Estate Tax, no tax need be paid to the Commonwealth of Pennsylvania, unless the decedent's Taxable Estate exceeds the current federal Tax Exclusion. But for Estates larger than the Exclusion value, Estate taxes will need to be paid to the federal government and to the Commonwealth of Pennsylvania. And that includes property that was owned by the decedent in another state; however the beneficiary is given credit for taxes paid on the property to the other state (72 P.S. 9117).

Both state and federal government do not tax property passing to the decedent's spouse, however, once the surviving spouse dies, all of his/her Estate is subject to Estate taxes. Setting up a Revocable Living Trust can significantly reduce the amount of taxes that need be paid once the surviving spouse dies.

THE UN-UNIFIED GIFT TAX

Up until the year 2002, if you gave someone more than $10,000 in any given year you had to report that gift to the IRS. The Annual Gift Tax Exclusion is now adjusted for the cost of living and is $11,000 for the year 2002. The IRS keeps count of amounts that you give over the Annual Gift Tax Exclusion. Although you are required to report the gift, no tax need be paid unless that running total is more than the federal Estate Tax Exclusion amount. If your running total does not exceed that amount during your lifetime, once you die, the cumulative value of gifts reported to the IRS will be added to your Taxable Estate.

Up until the change in the tax law in 2001, the Gift and federal Estate tax were unified. No Gift Tax needed to be paid unless the total value of the taxable gifts exceeded the federal Estate Tax Exclusion amount. That changes in 2004. In 2004, the federal Estate Tax Exclusion amount goes up to $1,500,000, but the amount for the Gift Tax Exclusion remains at $1,000,000, so they are no longer unified.

To summarize:
If you make a gift to anyone that is greater than the Annual Gift Tax Exclusion for that year, you must report the gift to the IRS. The IRS keeps a running count of gifts you made in excess of the Annual Gift Tax Exclusion. In 2004, if that sum exceeds $1,000,000, you will pay a federal Gift Tax on any amount that you give that is over the Annual Gift Tax Exclusion.

The federal Estate Tax is scheduled to be repealed in 2010, but not the federal Gift Tax.

At this time there is no Pennsylvania Gift Tax, but there is a **PENNSYLVANIA INHERITANCE TAX** on gifts, in excess of $3,000, made within a year of the decedent's death.

THE PENNSYLVANIA INHERITANCE TAX

The Commonwealth of Pennsylvania imposes an Inheritance Tax on transfers of property that take effect upon the death of a resident, or a non-resident who owns property in Pennsylvania. The Inheritance Tax is imposed on Non-Probate transfers such as property transferred to the survivor of a joint accout; a transfer to the beneficiary of anInter Vivos Trust, etc. Gifts made by the decedent within a year of his death that exceed $3,000 all also subject to the Inheritance Tax. Statute (72 P.S. 9107) gives a complete list of transfers that are subject to the tax. There are certain exemptions from this tax such as transfers to a spouse, or the proceeds of a life insurance policy. See Statue (72 P.S. 9111) for a complete list of transfers that are not subject to the Pennsylvania Inheritance Tax.

The rate of tax depends on the relationship of the beneficiary of the gift to the decedent. There is no tax for property inherited by the surviving spouse or a charity. Taxes for others are currently set at the following rate:

⇨ 4.5% for property inherited by the decedent's descendants (including adopted and step-children), parents grandparents, son-in-law, daughter-in-law.
⇨ 12% for property inherited by a brother or sister
⇨ 15% for everyone else   (72 P.S. 9116)

The state offers a 5% discount from the amount due if the Inheritance Tax is paid within three months of the death and a penalty if taxes are not paid within 9 months (72 P.S. 9142).

There are many deductions allowed, such as funeral expenses and the cost of the Probate procedure. A list of deductions appears in statutes 72 P.S. 9126 through 9130; however computing the actual Inheritance Tax due is complicated and will probably need the assistance of an attorney or an accountant.

GIVING WITH ONE HAND — TAKING WITH THE OTHER

The current federal Estate tax is scheduled to be phased out in the year 2010, but a new Capital Gains Tax is scheduled for 2010 that may prove even more costly than the Estate Tax. The new Capital Gains tax is related to the way inherited property is evaluated by the federal government. Real and personal property is inherited at a "step-up" in basis, meaning that if the decedent's property has increased in value from the time he acquired it, the beneficiary will inherit the property at its fair market value as of the decedent's date of death. For example, if the decedent bought stock for $20,000 and it is worth $50,000 as of his date of death, the beneficiary will take a step-up in basis of $30,000; i.e. the beneficiary inherits the stock at the current $50,000 value. If the beneficiary sells the stock for $50,000, he pays no Capital Gains tax. If the beneficiary holds onto the stock and later sells it for $60,000, the beneficiary will pay a Capital Gains tax only on the $10,000 increase in value since the decedent's death.

Up to 2009, there is no limit to the amount a beneficiary can take as a step-up in basis. But in 2010 caps are set in place. The decedent's Estate will be allowed a 1.3 million dollar step-up in basis, plus another 3 million for property passing to the surviving spouse (IRS Code 1022(b)). The new law could result in significant Capital Gains taxes that the beneficiary must pay. For example, suppose in 2010 you inherit a business from your father that he purchased for $100,000 and it is now worth 2 million dollars. There is a capital gain of 1.9 million dollars, but you are allowed a step-up in basis of only 1.3 million. If you sell it for 2 million dollars $600,000 of your inheritance will be subject to a Capital Gains tax.

We will discuss methods of reducing the Gift Tax and the Capital Gains Tax in Chapter 7.

MAYBE PROBATE ISN'T ALL THAT BAD

Although many methods can be used to transfer property without the need for Probate, it may be each method has a downside that is objectionable to you. Maybe you don't have enough money to warrant the cost of setting up the Trust at this time. Holding property jointly with another may raise issues of security and independence. Holding property so that it goes directly to a few beneficiaries in a Pay-On-Death account may not be as flexible as you wish. This is especially the case if you want to give gifts to several charities or to minor children.

For example, if you hold all your property so that it goes directly to your son without the need for Probate, and you ask him to use some of the money for your grandchild's education, it may be that your grandchild gets none of the money because your son is sued or falls upon hard times. If you keep your property in your name only and leave a Will giving a certain amount of money for your grandchild, the child will know exactly how much money you left and the purpose of that gift.

After taking into account all the pros and cons of avoiding Probate, you may well opt for a Will and a Probate procedure. If you make such a decision, it is important to keep in mind that Estate Planning is not an "all or nothing" choice. You can arrange your Estate so that certain items pass automatically to your intended beneficiary, and other items can be left in your name only, to be distributed as part of a Probate procedure. By arranging your finances in this manner, you can reduce the value of your Probate Estate, and that in turn should reduce the cost of Probate.

In the next chapter, we discuss the Will as an Estate Planning tool.

Those of you who have a Will may be thinking that there is no reason to read the Chapter, but does your Will:

- Make provision for the amount to be paid to your Personal Representative?
- Make gifts of your personal property? (jewelry, car, etc.)
- Name a Guardian to care for your minor child?
- Make adjustment for gifts or loans that you gave to the beneficiaries of your Will?
- Give specific instructions about how your bills and taxes are to be paid; i.e., which of your beneficiaries will have his inheritance reduced in order to pay your debts and taxes?

Has your Will been prepared so that it will be difficult for anyone to challenge it?

Have you stored your Will so that it is safe AND easily accessible to you during your lifetime and to your Personal Representative after your death?

If you answered "Yes" to all of the above questions, then you can skip over to Chapter 5.

Your Will – Your Way　　4

Many people decide that the Will is the best route to go but do not act upon it, thinking it unnecessary to prepare a Will until they are very old and about to die. But according to reports published by the National Center for Health Statistics (a division of the U.S. Department of Health and Human Services) 2 of every 10 people who die in any given year are under the age of 60. Twenty percent may seem like a small number until it hits close to home as it did with a young couple.

Alex and Cathy were an old-fashioned couple in a modern world. When they married, they knew they wanted a large family. There was no question that Cathy would stay home and raise the children while Alex went to work. Luckily he did very well as one of the managers of a string of restaurants. Better yet, he enjoyed his work. He loved to cook and would even take over the kitchen when he returned from work. That suited Cathy just fine because she had her hands full raising their three boys.

Cathy couldn't help thinking how lucky they were that morning as she fixed breakfast. A nice house. Healthy, if not rambunctious boys. All in all, a comfortable marriage. Her only concern that day was the fact that Alex was flying off on a business trip. All this terrorist news made her nervous about flying. Alex reassured her that it was only an hour's flight, and besides he was flying the company plane and not a commercial airliner.

But it was not terrorists that brought down the plane, just a malfunctioning rudder.

THINGS A WILL CAN DO

Though we all agree that one never knows, still people put off making a Will, figuring that if they die before getting around to it, Pennsylvania law will take over and their property will be distributed in the manner that they would have wanted anyway. The problem with that logic is the complexity of Pennsylvania's Laws of Intestate Succession. If you are survived by a spouse, child, parent or sibling, then it isn't too difficult to figure out who will inherit your property. But if none of these survive you, the ultimate beneficiary of your property may not be the person you would have chosen, had you taken the time to do so.

Others think that it is not necessary to have a Will because they have arranged their finances so that all of their property will be inherited without the need for Probate. But money could come into your Estate after your death. This could happen in any number of ways from winning the lottery and dying (of happiness, no doubt) to receiving insurance funds after your death. For example, if you die in a house fire, the company that insures your home may need to pay for damages done to the property. In such case, the funds will need to be paid to your Estate. A Personal Representative may need to be appointed and the insurance funds distributed according to Pennsylvania law.

If you die without a Will, the Personal Representative may not be the person you would have chosen. The monies may be distributed differently than you would have wished.

And there are other important reasons to make a Will.

📄 APPOINT PERSONAL REPRESENTATIVE

An important reason to make a Will is to appoint the person of your choice to serve as Personal Representative. Without a Will, the Court will appoint your spouse for the job. If you are unmarried, then whoever has the right to inherit your Estate can volunteer to serve as Personal Representative. If two or more are entitled to serve and there is a dispute over who should serve, then the Court makes the decision (20 Pa.C.S.A. 3155).

📄 SET PERSONAL REPRESENTATIVE'S FEE

Another important reason to make a Will is that you can come to an understanding with your Personal Representative about how much compensation he is to receive to settle your Estate. You can state that value in your Will.

⚠️ CAUTION — THE PERSONAL REPRESENTATIVE CAN SEEK MORE MONEY

You can put the amount of agreed compensation in your Will; however your Personal Representative can reject that amount and ask the Court to determine how much he should be paid. To avoid the problem, you can have your attorney draft an agreement that you and your Personal Representative sign and attach it to your Will. Having a separate fee agreement will not stop your Personal Representative from asking for more money, but with such an agreement, the Court will not agree to the increase unless something unusual occurs (such as a law suit) causing much more work than the ordinary Probate procedure.

You also need to keep in mind that the Personal Representative's fee is just to administer the Estate. It does not include payment for professional work he may do while settling the Estate. For example, if you appoint your attorney as Personal Representative, he can agree to the amount stated in the Will for his role as Personal Representative, and then ask the Court to award him attorney's fees as well.

Pennsylvania Courts have ruled that an attorney cannot "double dip," i.e., he can't charge for doing a certain job wearing his Personal Representative's hat; and then charge an additional sum for doing the same job as an attorney. But the Court did allow separate fees to be paid for different work (*Estate of Phillips*, 420 Pa.Super, 228 (1992), 616 A.2d 667).

The same goes for any other professional. If you appoint your accountant to serve as Personal Representative, he is entitled to receive compensation for his work as Personal Representative and also for any accounting work he does such as preparing and filing tax returns; preparing an inventory and doing an accounting for the beneficiaries.

A financial planner who serves as Personal Representative may be compensated for his management of the Estate property (buying and selling securities, taking care of rental property, etc.) in addition to his fee to administer the Estate. If you choose a professional to serve as Personal Representative, then have your compensation agreement specifically state what will be paid for duties performed in the administration of the Estate as Personal Representative and what monies will be paid as compensation for any professional service he performs.

📄 MAKE GIFTS OF YOUR PERSONAL PROPERTY

Another benefit to making a Will is that you can make provision for who will get your *personal property* (computers, antiques, securities, boats, snowmobiles etc.). When making a Will consider making provision for your car. If you make a specific gift of your car in your Will, it will be relatively simple for your Personal Representative to transfer the car to your beneficiary. If you do not make a specific gift of your car, then your Personal Representative will decide what to do with it. He may decide to sell it and include the proceeds of the sale in the Estate funds to be distributed as part of the Probate Estate; or he can give the car to one beneficiary of your Estate as part of that beneficiary's share of the Estate.

SMALL GIFTS MATTER

Many who have lost someone close to them report that the distribution of small personal items caused the greatest conflict. If you arrange your finances so that no Probate procedure is necessary, your next of kin will need to decide among themselves how to distribute your *personal effects* (clothing, books, music collection etc.). Without guidance from you and no Personal Representative with authority to make decisions, there could be disagreement and hard feelings, over items of little monetary value, but much sentimental value. If you make a Will, you can include a list of gifts of personal effects in your Will and your Personal Representative will distribute those gifts according to your list. Of course it is impossible to make a list of every item that you own; but you can instruct your Personal Representative to allow certain family members to take their choice of items not mentioned in your Will. If two or more family members want the same item, then have your Personal Representative use an appropriate lottery system (coin toss, high card in a cut of a deck of cards, etc.) to decide who "wins."

CAUTION: YOU CAN'T GIVE WHAT YOU DON'T HAVE

You need to give considerable thought whenever you make a *specific gift* to someone. It could be that you no longer own the item at the time of your death. This could happen with property or money. For example, suppose you leave all of your Estate to your son, with a specific gift of $10,000 to each of your three grandchildren. Your son is the *residuary beneficiary* of the Probate Estate, meaning he gets whatever is left once all of the bills are paid and all of the specific gifts made. If the cost of your last illness leaves your Probate Estate with only $30,000 to distribute, would you want the grandchildren to get their gifts and your son nothing? Of course the simple solution is to make all of them residuary beneficiaries by leaving each a percent of your Estate. For example, instead of making a specific gift to each grandchild you could leave 70% to your son and 10% to each grandchild.

NON-PROBATE ASSETS

You can make provision in your Will only for those items held in your name that do not transfer automatically to a named beneficiary upon your death. For example, property held in a Beneficiary Account, Trust property, IRA accounts, life insurance policies are all *Non-probate* assets because they will be inherited by your named beneficiary without the need for Probate. You have, in effect, already made a gift of these assets so unless you named your Estate as the beneficiary of these assets, they should not be mentioned in your Will. In fact, Pennsylvania statute (20 Pa.C.S.A. 6304(d)) states that an account with a right of survivorship or a beneficiary account cannot be changed by Will. This means that you cannot make a gift of that bank account in your Will. Upon your death, the bank will give the account to the surviving joint owner or to the named beneficiary, as the case may be.

MAKE ADJUSTMENT FOR PRIOR GIFTS

You can make adjustments in your Will for gifts or loans given during your lifetime. For example, if you loaned money to a family member and do not expect to be repaid, you can deduct the loan from that person's inheritance. There is no need to make the adjustment if the borrower gives you a promissory note because should you die, the monies will be owed to your Estate and the Personal Representative can deduct the monies owed from the borrower's inheritance. But if there is no evidence of the debt and you neglect to make a Will, the borrower will receive his full share as provided under the Laws of Intestate Succession.

That was the case with Sally and Tom. They were firm believers in treating each of their four children equally. "Share and share alike" was their favorite saying. Once Tom died, Sally continued with the tradition, never giving to one child, without giving something of equal value, to each of the other three.

Sally did not think of the loan she gave to her son as a gift. After all, he promised to pay it back, with interest. She did not ask her son to sign a promissory note. He was family. If you can't trust your own son, who can you trust?

The son was prompt with his monthly payments. But only two payments were made before his mother died suddenly, from a heart attack.

Sally never mentioned the loan to any of her other children. Neither did her son. Each child received one fourth of their mother's Estate; and none the wiser. Except whenever Sally's son dreams of his mother, she is not smiling.

MAKE PROVISION FOR PAYMENT OF DEBTS

Most Wills contain an instruction to the Personal Representative to ". . . pay all the expenses of my last illness, funeral expenses, costs of administration, taxes and just debts. . . " Under Pennsylvania law, paying all of your debts does not include paying off a loan on a gift made to a beneficiary.

For example, if you leave your car to a beneficiary, and you have a loan on the car, you need to specify whether you want the loan to be paid from your Probate Estate so that your beneficiary will inherit the car free and clear, or whether you want to have your beneficiary be responsible to pay off the loan. If you make no provision in your Will, then under Pennsylvania law, your beneficiary will inherit the loan along with the car (20 Pa.C.S. 2514).

This same rule applies even if you do not make a specific gift of the item. For example, if there is a mortgage on your home, and you make no mention of who is to inherit the home, then it will be inherited by your residuary beneficiaries; and they will be responsible to pay off the loan.

They can use the Estate funds to do so, but if there is not enough money in the Estate to pay off the loan, whoever takes title to the property will need to pay the debt or make arrangements to refinance the property.

MAKE PROVISION FOR PAYMENT OF TAXES

Taxes are another concern especially for those Estates large enough to be subject to Estate taxes. Unless you make some provision in your Will, your Personal Representative will pay Estate Taxes and Inheritance Taxes due on your Probate Estate from your Estate property. He will pay the taxes regardless of whether that tax is due because of a specific gift made to a beneficiary of your Estate or because of property left to a residuary beneficiary (20 Pa.C.S.A. 3702, 20 Pa.C.S.A. 3704, 72 Pa.C.S.A. 9144).

For example, suppose you leave a gift of $100,000 to be divided equally among your grandchildren, with the remainder of your Probate Estate to your spouse. That gift is subject to an Inheritance Tax of $4,500 (before applicable deductions). If you make no other provision, your grandchildren will inherit the full $100,000, and your spouse will inherit whatever is left after paying those taxes. If this is not as you wish, you can direct that the Inheritance Tax be paid by the beneficiary of the gift.

Those who inherit property through a Non-probate transfer (joint owner, beneficiary of your Trust, beneficiary of a Pay-On-Death account, beneficiary of a life insurance policy, etc.) are responsible to pay the tax on that transfer. If an Estate tax (federal or state) is due, the Personal Representative is responsible to file the Estate Tax return. He will ask the beneficiary of the Non-probate transfer to contribute his share of the taxes. If a beneficiary refuses to do so, the Personal Representative can ask the Court to apportion the taxes and then require the beneficiary to contribute his share (20 Pa.C.S.A. 3706).

Again, if this is not as you wish, you can include a provision in your Will (or your Trust) directing your Personal Representative to pay the taxes in the manner stated in your Will.

CHOOSE A GUARDIAN FOR YOUR MINOR CHILD

If one parent dies, then it is the right, and duty, of the surviving parent to care for the child. But it could happen that both parents become incapacitated or die before the child is grown. If you have a minor child, you can appoint someone to serve as the Guardian of the child in the event that both you and the other parent are deceased (20 Pa.C.S.A. 2519). You can even include a Trust in your Will, naming someone to serve as Trustee to care for property that you leave to your minor child.

See Chapter 7 for more information about how to make provision for the care of your minor child in the event of your incapacity, or death.

PREPARING YOUR WILL

After reading the last few pages those who do not have a Will may decide that a Will is a good thing to have and decide to sit down and write one out. And you can, because in the Commonwealth of Pennsylvania, you can prepare a Will in your own hand, without the assistance of an attorney. Such a Will is called a *holographic* Will.

But preparing a Will is like figure skating. It is harder than it looks. A Will needs to be clearly worded. A sentence that can be read in two different ways can lead to a dispute over what you intended; and that could lead to a long and expensive Court battle.

The Commonwealth of Pennsylvania allows an unwitnessed holographic Will to be admitted to Probate. However the problem with an unwitnessed Will is its authenticity. If no one sees you sign the Will, how do they know you actually wrote it out? It could be a forgery, or maybe someone was forcing you to sign it. The problem of authenticity can be solved by signing your Will in the presence of two witnesses and attaching an Affidavit to your Will in which you and the witnesses state, under oath, that at the time you signed the Will, you were

➢ at least 18 and of sound mind – and -

➢ under no undue influence

You can copy the form of the Affidavit from statute (20 Pa.C.S.A. 3132.1). Under Pennsylvania law, once you attach this Affidavit to your Will it becomes *Self-proved*, meaning that the Probate Court can accept your Will into Probate without the need for the testimony of any witness as to its authenticity.

CAN YOUR WILL BE CHALLENGED?

Even though a Will is Self-proved, it doesn't mean that it cannot be challenged. Especially if the witnesses to your Will are those who could profit from it. Someone could argue that you didn't know what you were doing when you signed the Will; i.e., you were not of sound mind and/or the witnesses pressured you into signing it; i.e. used undue influence.

But these things are not easily proven. Courts have ruled that a Will maker is of sound mind if:

- ☑ he knew what he was doing (namely making a Will); and

- ☑ he knew what property he had, and how he wanted to distribute his property; and

- ☑ he remembered who was dependent upon him and how they would be affected by his Will.

Just the fact that the Will maker's memory is impaired by age or disease, and can no longer conduct his business affairs, does not necessarily mean that he lacked the capacity to prepare a valid Will (*Estate of Richel*, 484 Pa.610 (1979), 400 A.2d 1268).

The Court in the above case also said that to prove undue influence whoever is challenging the Will must show that there was a confidential relationship between the Will maker and the beneficiary (close relative, spiritual advisor, attorney, doctor, financial advisor, etc.) AND there was a substantial benefit to that beneficiary AND the Will maker was of weakened intellect.

Even if there is no undue influence, and your Will is clearly worded, properly signed and witnessed, it can still be challenged if you are married and did not make provision for your spouse as required by Pennsylvania law. As explained in the last chapter, your spouse has the right to at least one third of your Estate. If your Will gives less than this amount your spouse has the right to elect against your Will.

Although your spouse has the right to elect against your Will, your adult children have no such right. You can give your child as much as you wish or nothing at all.

If you are concerned that someone may challenge your Will, it is important that you consult with an attorney who is experienced in Estate Planning. The attorney will prepare the Will according to your wishes. If you meet with the attorney in the privacy of his office, and without anyone else present, it will be difficult to prove that someone was using undue influence to force you to make gifts according to their wishes and not yours.

Once the Will is prepared according to your direction, the attorney can supervise the signing of your Will. He will see to it that your Will is signed and witnessed in the presence of two disinterested witnesses — usually members of his staff. Each witness will sign the Will next to your name as a witness; and they will sign a separate paragraph saying they saw you sign the Will, and you did so of your own free will and at the time you signed it you knew what you were doing.

Once signed in this manner it will be difficult for anyone to say that you did not know what you were doing when you signed the Will. If your Will is challenged your attorney will be able to present proof to the Court that the Will was prepared exactly as you wished, and that you had full capacity when you signed the Will. You can even have your attorney include a ***no contest*** provision in your Will stating that if your Will is challenged, whoever makes the challenge gets none of your Probate Estate.

Such a provision is called an ***In Terrorem Clause*** because it is designed to cause fear (if not terror) in the heart of your beneficiary. Many states will not enforce such a clause, because they want people to have the right to challenge a Will, and let the Court decide whether that challenge is proper. In Pennsylvania a provision that bars a challenge to your Will is not enforceable if the Court finds that there was ***probable cause*** ** for the challenge (20 Pa.C.S. 2521).

This law does not mean that you cannot include a "No Contest" provision in your Will. You can, and if you do, it may discourage frivolous law suits. Anyone who makes the challenge understands that if he loses, there is the chance that the Court will find that there was no good reason for making the challenge in the first place. Should the Court reach that conclusion, the Court will uphold the penalty provision and the person who made the challenge will be barred from inheriting anything under your Will. But the challenger also knows that if he wins, the Court must conclude that there was probable cause to bring the law suit. In that case, the In Terrorem Clause will not prevent him from inheriting property under your Will.

** Lawyer talk for "had good reason to do so."

STORING YOUR WILL

Once you sign your Will, you may wonder where to store it. If an attorney prepared your Will, he may suggest that he place it in his vault for safekeeping. By doing so, he ensures that your heirs will need to contact him as soon as you die. This does not mean that they are required to employ him should a Probate procedure be necessary. It only means that he will have an opportunity for future employment. In exchange, he gives you good value. Your Will is kept safely in his vault, and at sole cost to him.

Before allowing your attorney to store the Will, you need assurance that the attorney will be responsible for the document. You should get a receipt and something in writing that says:

⇨ The attorney accepts full responsibility for the storage of the Will. Should it be lost or damaged, he will replace the document at no cost to you; and if you are deceased, he will, at no cost to your heirs, present sufficient evidence to the Court to accept a valid copy of the Will into Probate.

⇨ There will be no charge to you, or your heirs, for the storage and retrieval of the document.

⇨ Should he sell his practice, retire, or die, he or the successor to his practice, will return the original document to you.

With all of this cost and liability, many attorneys will agree only to store a copy of your Will. In such case, consider storing your Will in a safe deposit box. You can keep the document in a fireproof safe deposit box within your home; and give a duplicate key to the person you have chosen to be your Personal Representative.

THE SAFE DEPOSIT BOX, SAFE BUT . . .

You might consider placing your document in a safe deposit box that you lease at a bank. The only problem with the bank safe deposit box is convenient access. If you hold a safe deposit box in your name only, then should you die, the bank will restrict access to the safe deposit box. Under Pennsylvania law, the bank may allow whoever has the key to your safe deposit box to inspect the contents of your safe deposit box provided they do so under the supervision of a bank officer or employee. The bank has the right to charge a reasonable fee for this service (72 P.S. 9192).

If your Will is there, they can forward it to the Probate Court. The bank will not allow anything else to be removed without Court authority. Once a Personal Representative is appointed by the Court, he will have such authority. The Personal Representative will need to schedule an appointment with the representative of the Pennsylvania Department of Revenue to be present when the safe deposit box is opened. The reason that the Department of Revenue representative needs to be present is to make an inventory of the contents of the safe deposit box (72 P.S. 9193).

Instead of making an appointment with the Department of Revenue representative, the Personal Representative can ask the bank to make an inventory of the contents of the safe deposit box. Again, the bank has the right to charge for this service.

Once the inventory is taken, your Personal Representative will be able to take possession of the contents of your safe deposit box.

This is a lot of work and expense, just to enable your beneficiaries to get the contents of your safe deposit box. If you arranged your finances to avoid Probate, it is self defeating to have entry to a safe deposit box trigger a Probate procedure.

For those who are married, the solution to the problem of accessing the safe deposit box after death, is to lease the box jointly with your spouse, such that each of you has free access to the box. Your spouse is not required to pay an Inheritance Tax, so there are no tax concerns for property she removes from the safe deposit box.

Regardless of where you choose to store your Will, let your Personal Representative know that you have a Will and how to retrieve it in the event of your death.

I thought you said a Will is not enough.

After reading this chapter, you may be thinking that the book is poorly named. After all, look at all the good things a Will can do:
* choose the person you want to settle your Estate
* arrange to have your Personal Representative settle your Estate for a reasonable fee
* give your personal items, including your car, to the person of your choice
* choose a Guardian for your child
* discourage a challenge to your Will.

But that is not all there is to an Estate Plan. A Will cares for your property when you are deceased, but it cannot provide for the care of your property in the event you become disabled. A complete Estate Plan provides for the care of your property during your lifetime and for the care of your person as well.

In these days of extended old age, many of us will need assistance with our health care and/or finances as we age. It is important to arrange to have someone manage finances and make medical decisions in the event that we are too aged or too ill to do so ourselves. These topics are covered in Chapters 8 and 9.

And a Will may be effective to transfer all that you own upon your death, but it cannot help your family pay for your debts. It may be that you have so many debts that your family is left with little or nothing. A complete Estate Plan provides for the financial well being of your family once you are deceased; and that is the topic of the next chapter.

Arranging To Pay Bills   5

You can think of your Estate Plan as being composed of two separate parts, a Lifetime Plan and an Inheritance Plan. Your Lifetime Plan concerns the care of your property during your lifetime, with the goal being maximum control and protection. Your Inheritance Plan concerns the inheritance of your property, with the goal being minimum cost and hassle to your beneficiaries. You could consider your Estate Plan to be a master plan that balances the goals of the Lifetime Plan with those of the Inheritance Plan.

When people consider their Inheritance Plan, they are mostly concerned about giving their possessions away. Many do not take into account how the bills they have accumulated will be paid once they are deceased, or even who will be responsible for paying those bills. Most of us do not worry about providing for the payment of our debts, thinking "I'll have that paid off long before I die." But with easily available credit, many are maintaining a high debt balance as a way of life. Paying off all of their loans is not a priority. Many will live their lives without ever being free of debt.

This does not imply that people do not know how to manage their funds. For many people (and corporations), it makes good sense to use other people's money to carry on business. In fact, great debt is a badge of honor for the wealthy. If a bank will lend you a million dollars, it means you have the means to repay that amount. Banks will not lend much money to those with few assets. Rich or poor, we all need to think about how our debts will be paid once we are gone.

WHO IS RESPONSIBLE TO PAY BILLS?

Suppose you die without funds, and owing money. Does the debt die with you or is someone else responsible to pay what you owe? If you are married, the first person the creditor will look to, is your spouse. To understand the basis of this expectation, you need to know a bit of the history of our legal system.

Our laws are derived from the English Common Law. Under English Common law, a single woman had the right to own property in her own name and also the right to contract to buy or sell property. When a woman married, her legal identity merged with her spouse. She could not hold property free from her husband's claim or control. She could no longer enter into a contract without her husband's permission.

Once married, a woman became financially dependent on her husband. He, in turn, became legally responsible to provide his wife with basic necessities — food, clothing, shelter and medical services. If anyone provided basic necessities to his wife, then, regardless of whether the husband agreed to be responsible for the debt, he became obliged to pay for them. This law was called the **DOCTRINE OF NECESSARIES**.

In the United States, a series of Married Women's Rights Acts were passed giving a married woman the right to own property. Under Pennsylvania law, a married woman has the right to contract, own and transfer property, the same as does a single woman (21 P.S. 82).

As Married Women's Rights laws were passed state to state, a series of cases tested whether the Doctrine of Necessaries still applied in that state.

Questions that judges had to decide were:
If a wife can own property and contract to pay for her own necessities, should her husband be responsible for such debts in the event she does not have enough money to pay for them?

And if the husband is responsible to pay for his wife's necessities should she be responsible for his?

In Pennsylvania the answer was "yes" to both questions. (*Porter v Karivalis,* 718 A.2d 823 (Pa.Super. 1998). The Court ruled that both married partners are responsible to pay for the support and maintenance of the family, but the creditor must first try to collect from the person who ran up the bill. That means the creditor must sue the partner who contracted for the necessities. If the creditor obtains the judgment but is unable to collect because the contracting spouse has no money, then the creditor can collect the money from the non-contracting partner.

This right continues after death. If a person dies owing money for necessities, his Estate is responsible to pay that debt. If the decedent was married and there is not enough money in his Estate to pay that debt, then in Pennsylvania, the creditor has the right to seek payment from the surviving spouse, regardless of whether the spouse agreed to pay the bill.

Which leads to the next question. Is anyone other than your spouse responsible to pay monies you owe? For joint debts, the answer is "yes."

JOINT DEBTS

A *joint debt* is a debt that two or more people are responsible to pay. Usually the contract or promissory note reads that both parties agree to *joint and several* liability, meaning they both agree to pay the debt and each of them, individually, agree to pay the debt. A joint debt can also be in the form of monies owed by one person with payment guaranteed by another person. If the person who owes the money does not pay, then the *guarantor* (the person who guaranteed payment) is responsible to pay the debt.

Should you die, your hospital bills, nursing home bills, funeral expenses, legal fees incurred because of the death are all debts of your Estate. They are not joint debts unless someone guaranteed payment for the monies owed. Hospital and nursing home bills are considered to be necessities, so if you are married and there are insufficient funds in the Estate to pay for these bills, then your spouse is responsible for payment, regardless of whether your spouse agreed to be jointly liable for the debt.

JOINT SPOUSAL DEBTS
A surviving spouse may need to pay for the decedent's necessities, but not for any other debt unless the debt was joint. Your spouse is responsible to pay for loans signed by both of you. For example, if you both are authorized to use a credit card, and there is no money in your Estate, then your spouse must pay the debt. Property taxes are a joint debt if you and your spouse both own the property.

JOINT PROPERTY BUT NO JOINT DEBT

Suppose you have a credit card in your name only, and you have a bank account together with your son. Should you die, can the credit card company require that half of the monies in the account be used to pay the debt?

The answer to this question depends on how the account is titled. If it is a ***Joint Tenancy*** account, then there are ***rights of survivorship***. Upon your death, your son will own the account 100%. He will not be responsible to pay any of your debts from that account. His only responsibility will be to pay any Inheritance or Estate Tax that may be due as a result of his inheritance of your share of the account (20 Pa.C.S.A. 6304).

If the account is held as ***Tenants-In-Common***, then there are no rights of survivorship. As soon as the bank learns of the death, they will freeze the Tenancy In Common account, until a Personal Representative is appointed to take possession of the decedent's property. Your son will continues to own his share of the account. Your share of the account becomes part of your Probate Estate, and as such is available to pay your debts.

JOINT PROPERTY — JOINT DEBT

Of course, it's a different story if you held the credit card jointly with your son. Should one of you die, the other is responsible to pay the bill regardless of who ran up the bill. The bill can be paid from the Joint account or from any other account owned by the surviving debtor.

PAYING FOR CREDIT CARD DEBT

Most of us are wise enough not to hold a credit card jointly with a child, but we do not hesitate to hold a credit card together with our spouse, especially if we are using the card to pay for necessities. If paying that bill could be a struggle for the surviving spouse, you might consider credit card insurance to cover the debt.

Many credit card companies offer insurance policies and include the premium as part of the monthly payment. It benefits the credit card company to offer life insurance as part of the credit package, because they are assured of prompt payment should the borrower die.

Of course, in these days of high credit card interest rates, you and your spouse may be struggling to pay your monthly credit charge. Adding still another charge to the account may not be an option, regardless of the security offered to your spouse. In such case, a better route might be for you to remove your name from the account and open a new account in your name only. This is especially important if you are using your credit card to pay for your business expenses, and not family necessities. Your surviving spouse is not responsible to pay for your business debts unless your spouse agreed to do so.

Still another reason not to hold a joint credit card is that each of you can establish your own line of credit in the event one of you retires or is out of work. Should the breadwinner of the family die, it may be difficult for the surviving spouse to establish credit if the spouse is retired and/or has no recent work record. It is easier for an unemployed spouse to establish a line of credit when he/she is married to someone who is working.

OTHER TYPES OF LOAN INSURANCE

Most mortgage companies offer mortgage insurance to their borrowers. Mortgage rates are currently low, so an additional charge for mortgage insurance on the life of the primary wage earner may be worth the effort. This is particularly the case with families raising children. With such insurance, the family can inherit the homestead free of debt. The monthly insurance charge may be a small price to pay to ensure that the children can continue to live in their own home until they are grown.

Car loan insurance is still another thing to consider. If a married couple purchases (or leases) a car, and one of them dies, it may be a struggle for the other to pay off the loan. This was the case with Eva and Howard. Both had to work to support their three children. They owned two well used cars. It seemed that one car or the other was always in the shop. When they saw a "NO INTEREST" advertisement for a new car, they decided the offer was too good to pass up.

The monthly payments were high, but it was their only luxury. With both their salaries, they were able to make the payments. When Howard had his first heart attack, he was out of work for several weeks so they struggled to keep the payments current. Howard worked in construction, and was anxious to return to work. The doctors advised that such work might be too strenuous for his weakened heart. Construction work was all Howard knew, and the pay was good, so he ignored the warning and went back to his old job.

The second heart attack was fatal, leaving Eva as the sole means of support for her family.

With Howard gone there was no need for two cars. Eva could not afford the payments on the new car anyway, so she decided to sell it. Unfortunately, what she could get for the car was significantly less than the balance owed. Once she fell behind in payments she decided to surrender the car rather than have them repossess it. She was sure they would understand, considering all that she had been through these past several months, not to mention that she was a widow with three small children.

They didn't understand.

The company took the car and then sued for the balance of monies owed. The judge was sympathetic, but under the law there is no "life is tough" defense. He ruled that Eva had to pay the monies owed; and, as per the terms of the loan agreement, she even had to pay the fees for the company's attorney and all court costs. What an emotional and financial nightmare!

The pity was, it all could have been avoided, had they worked payment of debts into their Estate Plan. Howard was the primary driver of the new car and the primary wage earner. All he had to do was to put the loan in his name only, and take out loan insurance. Eva would have inherited the car, debt free. She could have kept it or sold it as she saw fit.

Even if Howard didn't purchase loan insurance, had he put the loan in his name only, the company could only have sued his Estate. They would not have been able to sue Eva personally.

PURCHASING LIFE INSURANCE

The good part of purchasing loan insurance — be it credit card insurance, mortgage insurance or car insurance, is that you can usually purchase the insurance without taking a medical examination. The down side is that companies generally do not offer such insurance to those over the age of 65; and for those under 65 the cost of the insurance is a factor. It usually costs more to purchase loan insurance than a life insurance policy. Those in fairly good health need to comparison shop. If it is your goal to have insurance cover all of your outstanding debts, then the cost of a single life insurance policy may be much less than purchasing several loan insurance policies.

The Estate Planning strategy of purchasing life insurance to pay off all of your loans works best if you are married and your spouse is jointly liable for your debts. If you name your spouse as beneficiary of the life insurance policy, he/she can use the life insurance funds to pay off all monies owed.

If you name your spouse, child, or a relative who is dependent on you for support, as beneficiary of your insurance policy, and that person has no legal obligation to pay your debts, then none of your creditors can ask your beneficiary to use the insurance funds to pay your debts.

If you name anyone else as beneficiary of your life insurance policy, then the proceeds of the insurance policy are available to pay your debts (42 Pa.C.S.A. 8124).

If you want the insurance funds used to pay your debts, then you need to name your Estate as beneficiary of your policy. If you want someone to inherit money after you are gone, and you do not want those funds reduced by the cost of Probate or to pay off your debts, then naming that person as beneficiary of the insurance proceeds should accomplish your goal.

With or without debt, you may be wondering about life insurance — should you have it? How much is enough? The answer to these questions depends on the "sleep at night" factor, namely how much insurance do you need so that you won't worry about insurance coverage when you go to sleep at night? It is often more an emotional than a financial issue.

Some people have an "every man for himself" attitude and are content to have no life insurance at all. When they die, whatever they have, they have. And that is what their heirs will inherit. Others worry about how their loved ones will manage if they are not around to support them, and decide to purchase enough insurance to maintain their dependents in their accustomed life style. The same person may have different thoughts about insurance coverage as their circumstances change — from no coverage in his bachelor days to more-than-enough coverage in his child rearing days to just-enough-to-bury-me in his senior years.

Insurance companies recognize that people's needs change over the years. Many companies offer flexible insurance coverage. As with any consumer item, it is a good idea to shop around. In addition to the problem of how much life insurance to carry, there is the concern of how the monies will be spent. Leaving a large sum of money to a person who is less than prudent, may lead to a spending spree.

ANNUITIES TO SPREAD THE INHERITANCE

Most beneficiaries go through their inheritance within two years. For many, the reason the money is gone so soon, is that there just wasn't much money to inherit in the first place. But for others, it's a spending frenzy. Luckily, people are fairly consistent in their spending habits, so you probably know in advance whether your intended beneficiary will "go wild," or prudently invest the monies he inherits.

If you want to leave an insurance policy benefit to someone you love, but the intended beneficiary is immature, or a born spendthrift, then a simple solution to the problem may be to purchase an *Annuity* rather than a life insurance policy with a single lump sum payment. An annuity is a type of insurance policy that can be set up so that your beneficiary (the *Annuitant*) receives money on a regular basis (monthly, quarterly, yearly) rather than one large payment upon your death.

Hopefully, this regular source of income will encourage your beneficiary to think ahead, and learn to budget his finances. In addition to spreading out the inheritance, you can protect some of the monies from the claims of the creditors of your beneficiary. In Pennsylvania, up to $100 per month of monies received by your beneficiary under an annuity contract is exempt from the claims of his creditors (42 Pa.C.S.A 8124).

This means that the creditor cannot force the insurance company to pay the first $100 to the creditor instead of the beneficiary. Of course, once the beneficiary receives the annuity, he can use some, or all of those monies to pay any debt he may owe.

THINGS THAT CAN BE INHERITED DEBT FREE

Pennsylvania is a state that respects the rights of creditors. There are few items that can be inherited by your beneficiary free of the claims of your creditors. As discussed, your spouse, child, or dependent relative can inherit the proceeds of your life insurance policy free from the claims of your creditors. And that is so, regardless of the value of the life insurance policy (42 Pa.C.S.A. 8124).

THE FAMILY EXEMPTION

Your surviving spouse is also entitled to keep up to $3,500 of your real or personal property. If you have no surviving spouse, then any child who was living with you is entitled to this Family Exemption. If you have no spouse or child but your parent (or parents) were living with you then they are entitled to this Family Exemption (20 Pa.C.S.A. 3121).

This Family Exemption is inherited free from the claims of your creditors, with the exception of any money that might be needed for the administration of your Probate Estate (20 Pa.C.S.A. 3392).

✧ RETIREMENT PLANS ✧

Any pension or annuity paid to you by an employer or a private corporation is exempt from the claims of your creditors, provided the pension is not assignable. If you have such a plan, and it provides for your benefits to continue to be paid to another after your death, then those funds are not available to your creditors.

Monies you hold in a Federal retirement plans 401(a), 403 a & b, 408 (IRA accounts), 409 or 530 are exempt from the claims of your creditors provided you did not contribute more that $15,000 to the plan in any given year. Any amount in excess of $15,000 is available to pay your debts. If you did not contribute more than $15,000 in any given year, then all monies received by beneficiaries of these plans are protected from the claims of your creditors (42 Pa.C.S. 8124 (b)).

NO EXEMPTION FOR TAXES

In general, income taxes are not paid when money is placed in a retirement plan. Taxes are paid when the monies are withdrawn from the account regardless of whether the monies are withdrawn by the retiree or the person he named as beneficiary of the retirement plan. If your beneficiary inherits money from your pension, retirement allowance, or annuity, he may need to pay taxes on those monies.

AN ESTATE PLAN FOR THE BANKRUPT

You may think the above title to be an oxymoron (a contradiction in terms). If a person is bankrupt, why plan for an Estate he doesn't have? But facts are, that people who file for bankruptcy are often quite wealthy and that is their downfall. Because they have substantial income or property, banks and people are willing to lend them money. If more money is borrowed than can be repaid, the unhappy result is bankruptcy. In the event you are concerned about meeting your responsibilities as parent or spouse, yet you enjoy a life style of financial brinksmanship, then consider investing in items that are "creditor proof."

That's exactly what Alan decided to do. Alan was astute, well aware of his strengths and weaknesses. He enjoyed his work and knew he had the capacity to earn large sums of money. But he also knew he was a gambler. Not the Las Vegas type, but a gambler in business ventures. "No risk, no gain" was one his favorite sayings.

If you charted Alan's net worth over the years it would look like the peaks and valleys of the NASDAQ. Lots of high highs and low lows. Unfortunately, he married a woman who did not share his adventurous spirit. His wife became increasingly intolerant of their financial instability. She came to realize that this was his life style and things would never change. "All gamblers die broke," she said as she walked out the door with their 5 year old daughter in tow.

That, and the fact that he had to declare bankruptcy, brought Alan up short; and he began to be concerned about his future and that of his family.

Alan talked things over with his bankruptcy attorney "I am a good businessman, but not a clairvoyant. There was no way to predict the turn of events that led to this situation. But I know I will bounce back, and it will just be a matter of time before I earn my next fortune. I also know that I am an entrepreneur and not a 9 to 5 type guy so this could happen again. What concerns me is how to provide some security for my child in case something happens to me before she is grown."

His attorney's response was a surprise.
"Move to another state."

"You're kidding."

"Not really. There are few items in Pennsylvania that are creditor proof. Many states have homestead creditor protection, so at least you can keep a roof over your head. A homestead in Texas or Florida is protected 100% — even if it is worth a million dollars. We have no homestead protection here in Pennsylvania. Your creditors could force the sale of your home to pay for even a small amount of money that you owe. You could put money into a federal retirement plan such as an IRA or Keogh account, and your daughter would inherit that free of your debts. There are some exceptions. Any money you put into your account within one year of filing for bankruptcy is not protected from your creditors, nor is any amount that you put into the account that exceeded $15,000 in any given year (42 Pa.C.S.A 9124)."

Alan didn't think that would work. "I am my own boss, and I don't have the self discipline to put money aside each month for my retirement."

The attorney explained "You can purchase a life insurance policy with your wife or daughter as beneficiary. Regardless of the value of the policy, they would inherit the proceeds free of your debts. The only problem with an insurance policy, is that the cash value of the policy is available to your creditors during your lifetime (42 Pa.C.S.A. 8124) .

Alan was annoyed "You're saying that here in Pennsylvania, while I am alive, all I can protect are my retirement funds? What about all those millionaires who protect their money in offshore Trusts? If I really hit it big, why can't I do that?"

"You could, but there are many drawbacks. Just to set up an offshore Trust costs tens of thousands of dollars, not to mention how much it would cost just to maintain the Trust."

Alan said "Yes, but if I had millions of dollars that would not be a problem."

"True, but there are other considerations. Once you put your money into the Trust, you are essentially giving up control of that money."

Alan was skeptical "Oh come now. Why would anyone put his money where he can't get to it?"

The attorney explained "The Trust can be set up so that funds are available for whatever the millionaire wants. Usually funds are made available to support his family. Trust funds can be used to maintain the family home or yacht. Monies from the Trust can be used to pay for travel or for an expensive vacation. And of course the Trust would provide for the transfer of the property to the millionaire's beneficiaries, once the millionaire dies."

The attorney continued "What the millionaire can't do is be the Trustee of the Trust. The millionaire cannot be Trustee, because if he were, he would have control over the money, and his creditors could take legal action here in the United States to force him to use his Trustee powers to use that money to pay his creditors."

"How can they force the issue? Why couldn't he, as Trustee, just refuse?"

"Remember, that as long as the millionaire is a citizen of the United States, and he is physically present in the states, he is subject to the laws of this country. If a creditor goes to Court and wins, the U. S. Judge could order the millionaire, as Trustee, to use Trust funds to pay that debt. If the millionaire-Trustee refused, the Judge could put him in jail for contempt of Court. No, for an offshore Trust to work, the Trust must be a foreign Trust, that is, drafted according to the laws of a foreign country, Trust property must be located outside of the United States, and the Trustee cannot be a citizen of the United States."

Alan said "Well I guess the millionaire might have a relative who is not a U.S. citizen to manage the Trust."

The attorney agreed "Yes, or he could use a financial institution that does not do business in the U.S., to manage the funds. But there are other problems with an offshore Trust. There's the safety factor. Trust funds are kept outside of the United States. If the funds are kept in a foreign bank and the country suffers an economic collapse, then those funds could be lost."

Alan wondered "Isn't that much the same risk as money in a U.S. bank? Only $100,000 of the cash in a U. S. bank account is insured. If the bank fails, any money in that bank over $100,000 could be lost."

The attorney disagreed "Our U.S government is stable, and we trust that they will regulate U.S. banks and keep our money safe. But that is not the case with other small countries. The government of a small country could collapse and the banks along with it."

"But why keep money in a bank? Most millionaires have their funds invested in stocks and bonds, or in real property."

The attorney agreed "True, but real estate could be risky. If your Trust contains real property located within the United States, your creditor could go to a U.S. court and take that property."

Alan wondered "Couldn't the creditor take the overseas property as well?"

"He could, but it would be hard. For one thing he would need to find the property. And the Trustee is not about to tell him where it is, unless the creditor sues, and the laws of that foreign country require the Trustee to tell. Even if the creditor locates Trust property, whether it is stocks, bonds, or real estate, most offshore Trusts are established in countries that are not creditor friendly. For example, if you set up an off shore Trust in the Cook Islands, they will not accept a judgment that a creditor got in the United States. The creditor will need to employ a Cook Islands attorney to sue you all over again in the Cook Islands. That's expensive. And the Cook Islands have a higher standard of proof. Here in the U.S., all your creditor need do is to show that you owe the money *by a preponderance of the evidence.* That's lawyer talk for "the jury must be more than 50% sure you owe the money."

In the Cook Islands, the creditor's attorney must prove you owe the money *beyond a reasonable doubt* (Cook Islands, International Trusts Act of 1984 Section 13B(1)). That standard is the one we use here in the U.S. for criminal cases. In addition, the foreign country usually has a short Statute of Limitations, so if your creditor does not sue you in that country within that period of time, he cannot sue you at all."

Alan said "I can see why offshore Trusts are so popular."

The attorney cautioned "But there are other problems. The U.S. considers transfers into and/or out of the Trust to be taxable. The IRS requires special tax returns to be filed for all foreign Trusts. In addition, the IRS looks closely at offshore Trusts to determine whether they are fraudulent transfers, designed to avoid U.S. income taxes or U.S. Estate taxes. The IRS wants to be sure that the creditor the millionaire is avoiding isn't Uncle Sam!"

Alan said "Yes, but if you pay your taxes, that shouldn't be a problem. If I ever get to the point where I am that wealthy, then we'll come back and discuss setting up an offshore Trust."

The attorney refused "No, I'm just a country lawyer. If you want to go that route, you need a specialist — someone who has overseas connections, and who has experience in writing such Trusts. If you are serious about setting up an offshore Trust, let me know and I will recommend someone to you."

"O.K. I will."

The attorney offered a final word of caution "If you are able to accumulate a significant amount of money, don't risk it all in a business venture. Limit the amount of money you can lose to just the money that you invest in business. Keep your personal funds separate and protected from your business debts. If you want to start a business, make sure that you cannot be personally liable for your business debts. You can avoid personal liability by forming a corporation, or a Limited Partnership, or a Limited Liability Company.** Stay away from a sole proprietorship or a business partnership."

** These topics are discussed in the next chapter.

Your Business Estate Plan 6

It would take a very thick book to do justice to the topic of Business Estate Planning. Estate Planning issues must be discussed for each type of business:

CONTROL　　How to control and protect your business during your lifetime.

BENEFICIARY　How to be sure your business goes to the beneficiary of your choice.

COST　　How to transfer your business to your beneficiary quickly and at lowest cost.

With just one chapter to devote to the topic, we can only provide the reader with an overview of the subject. Hopefully, the overview will give the reader some ideas that can later be pursued with an attorney.

We have written this chapter for the reader who listed a business value as part of his Net Worth on page 4. People who are self employed, but who do not think of themselves as business owners, may profit from the information covered in this chapter, as well.

This chapter should also be of interest to someone who has the possibility of inheriting a business interest, such as the child of a small business owner, or perhaps the spouse of someone who is self employed. Even those who are thinking of starting a business, may find it worthwhile to take a few minutes to read this chapter.

Those who have no present business interest may want to skip this chapter and go on to Chapter 7.

TRANSFERRING THE FAMILY BUSINESS

Your business is your property, and as such it is included as part of your overall Estate Plan. But owning a business isn't as simple as just holding title to a tangible item such as a car or parcel of real estate. For example, if you own a business in your name only, i.e. as a ***sole proprietor***, there may be no single document that indicates ownership of your business property. You probably filed a Fictitious Name Registration in the county where you conduct business and with the Pennsylvania Department of State (54 Pa.C.S.A. 303, 311).

The Fictitious Name Registration states the name and address of the business and the name and address of the owner of the business; but it does not identify business property. You could have trucks, computers, copiers or other expensive business equipment. Title to business property is probably held in your own personal name.

The business bank account may be in your name only, or in the name of the business with you alone as signatory on the account. Charge cards and business loans are either in your name only, or in your name as guarantor.

If you want to leave your business to your son, how do you do it? Do you leave him the equipment used in the business? If you have a business name that you have not registered, how do you give him that name? And how do you handle business related loans? If you leave him the business, will he agree to be responsible for any outstanding business debt?

Partnerships can be even more complicated, unless there is a written partnership agreement that says how the business is to be transferred in the event that one of the partners dies. Even the transfer of a corporation can be a major headache if there are several shareholders and no shareholder's agreement to say how shares should be transferred in the event of the death or incapacity of the shareholder.

For these reasons, it is important to think about an Estate Plan for your business. You need to ask yourself:

> *How can I have maximum protection and control over my business during my lifetime?*
>
> *How can I structure my business so that it can be transferred quickly and at minimum cost?*

We will examine each type of business ownership as it relates to the above questions.

WHAT'S THE BEST TYPE OF BUSINESS OWNERSHIP?

Those who read the first five chapters know us well enough not to expect a definitive answer to the above question. Our job, as we see it, is to explain the rules of the game (i.e., Pennsylvania law) to the reader. Once you know how things work in Pennsylvania, you can make an informed decision as to the type of business ownership that best accomplishes your goal.

> **SOLE PROPRIETORSHIP**
> Maximum control — Maximum liability

You are the boss if you do business in your name only, but you take full personal responsibility for any loss suffered by the company; and as explained, you may need to consult with an attorney if you want to make arrangements for someone to take over your business should you become incapacitated or die.

Because of this personal liability issue, many people think it best to form a corporation as soon as they start up the business. That may not be the best strategy. It takes money to form a corporation. You may need to pay an attorney to set up the corporation. You will need to file a Certificate of Incorporation with the Pennsylvania Secretary of State and pay a filing fee (currently $100). Each year you need to file an annual report with the Pennsylvania Department of Revenue (72 P.S. 1895, 72 P.S. 7403, 15 Pa.C.S.A 153).

And there may be additional accounting fees, because you will need to file separate corporate income tax returns; one for the Commonwealth of Pennsylvania and one for the IRS.

You do not need to pay filing fees to the Secretary of State to form a sole proprietorship, and you do not need to file separate income tax returns. You can include your business income as part of your personal income tax return and not go through the cost and hassle of filing a separate corporate return.

Another reason to start business as a sole proprietorship is the risk of failure. Although every new business owner thinks his venture must surely culminate in riches, research conducted by the Brandow Company shows that only 55% of new businesses get to celebrate their third birthday (see their data at www.brandow.com). You can always form a corporation should your business succeed. If the business does not succeed, then at least you didn't waste time, effort and money to form a corporation.

But What About My Personal Liability?
Many people seek to limit their personal liability by forming a corporation, however, that doesn't always work in the real world. For example, if you wish to rent a store front or office space, the experienced landlord will allow you to lease the space in the corporate name, but he will require you to sign as a guarantor. That means that should the business fail, he has the right to sue you, personally, for the full value of the lease. Once you have established a successful business, the landlord may agree to just hold the business liable; and in that case having a corporation instead of a sole proprietorship does limit your personal liability.

Regardless of what form of business ownership you choose, you can be held personally liable for any fraudulent or negligent act that you commit. The way to avoid personal liability for fraudulent acts is not to willfully (deliberately) deceive or cheat anyone.

Most of us are honest folk, but negligence is another matter. We all goof. The way to limit your liability for negligence is to purchase insurance that provides protection for mistakes and accidents. For example, if you open a title insurance business, you can purchase an Error and Omissions insurance policy to cover a loss caused by a mistake you might make in a title search. If you have any business involving the care of a person (adult or child day care center, nurse practitioner, etc.), it is important to have coverage for an injury to a client due to accident or malpractice.

If you have a business location (a storefront or office) consider purchasing a comprehensive business insurance policy to cover injury to anyone who visits your business, as well as damages to the premises. For example, if you open a flower shop you can get insurance to cover an injury to a customer who slips and falls. The same policy can cover vandalism to your shop, such as a broken plate glass window. You can be compensated for loss should a storm cause the electricity to go out and your shipment of fresh cut flowers wilt for lack of refrigeration.

The purpose of any business insurance policy is to shift the risk of a business loss from your pocket to that of the insurance company.

And the downside is . . .
The problem with insurance is the greater the risk, the greater the cost. We all would like 100% insurance coverage, but few of us can afford the premium. What holds true for life insurance holds true for business insurance. The right amount of insurance coverage for you is the amount that allows you to sleep at night.

> **BUSINESS PARTNERSHIP**
> Shared control — Maximum liability

A business partnership is much like a marriage. You can both start out with the best of intentions, only to find that you are hopelessly incompatible. The break-up of a business partnership can be just as bitter and hotly contested as the breakup of a marriage. A properly drafted Partnership Agreement is a must — not only to set the terms of a dissolution, but to clearly state what is expected of each partner; i.e., how much each will contribute to the business venture in terms of effort or financing.

The Partnership Agreement should cover what will happen to the partner's share in the event of his incapacity or death. Most Partnership Agreements provide for an appraisal of the business and the buy out of the deceased (or disabled) partner's share. The Partnership Agreement may need to be backed up with financing. For example, you could sign a Partnership Agreement that requires the company to buy out your partnership interest should you become disabled or die. But what good is the Agreement if there is not enough cash in the company to pay for the buy out?

You will have better protection if the Partnership Agreement requires the company to maintain disability and life insurance to pay for the buy out. Many insurance companies offer Key man insurance. The policy is designed to compensate the company for the loss of someone who is essential to the continuation of the business. If sufficient insurance is purchased, the proceeds of the policy can be used to cover any loss suffered by the company and to buy out the share of the company that was owned by the deceased or disabled partner.

COMPANIES THAT LIMIT LIABILITY

The sole proprietorship and the partnership are the earliest type of business organization. Pennsylvania laws governing these types of business organizations have their roots in English Common Law. Common law requires the sole proprietor and each business partner to take full personal responsibility for the debts of the company. As people became ever more litigious (lawyer talk for "sue happy") businessmen sought to limit their liability and prevailed on the legislature to create a form of business ownership to limit that liability.

Legislatures in each state responded to that need by giving businessmen the right to create a company (the corporation) with an identity separate from the owners of the business. By doing business as a corporation, the businessman's liability is limited to the money he invests in the company. A person can sue the corporation for business debts, but not the owners of the corporation.

This does not mean that a corporate owner can use the corporation to do things that are fraudulent. If he does, he can be held personally liable. The owner of the corporation cannot use the corporation as a "veil" to cover his wrongdoing. The law will not allow a company to use the corporate structure as a shield for illegal or wrongful conduct. Pennsylvania courts have ruled that they can disregard the corporate forms and "pierce the corporate veil" whenever justice and public policy demand (*Wicks v. Milzoco Builders, Inc.*, 470 A.2d 86 (Pa. 1983)).

THE CORPORATION
flexible control — limited liability

Whoever forms a corporation (the *incorporator*) has maximum control over the corporation. He decides how the company will operate by having the Articles of Incorporation and the company By-laws prepared according to his specifications. He can keep full control of the company as the only shareholder, or he can distribute shares and give up as much control as he wishes.

Transferring corporate ownership is simple. It is a matter of signing a stock certificate transferring the shares of stock in the company. If you own shares of stock in your name only, then upon your death, your Personal Representative will transfer the shares according to your Will, or if no Will, according to the Laws of Intestate Succession. But keeping shares in your name only, may not be the best way to go if you own a majority of shares and operate the business yourself. If Probate is necessary, it may take several months before the shares are transferred to the proper beneficiary, meanwhile, someone needs to continue to operate the business. If you do not leave specific directions for the continuance of the business, the Personal Representative (or the Orphans' Court) may decide it best to just sell the company and give the proceeds of the sale to your beneficiaries.

The better route is to have your attorney prepare a Revocable Living Trust and transfer the shares into the Trust. The Trust document can give your Successor Trustee specific instructions about how the business is to be managed or transferred should you become incapacitated or die. Still another important benefit is to avoid the need to Probate what may be your only valuable asset.

THE LIMITED PARTNERSHIP

Just as a sole proprietor can limit his liability by forming a corporation, the partners of a general partnership can limit their liability by converting the partnership to a **Limited Partnership**. As with the corporation, the Limited Partnership is a creation of the legislature and is regulated by Pennsylvania law. A Certificate of Limited Partnership must be filed with the Pennsylvania Department of State (15 Pa.C.S.A 8511).

The structure of a Limited Partnership differs from a general partnership. In a general partnership, each partner has full authority to conduct business on behalf of the partnership. Each partner is personally liable for monies owed by the partnership, regardless of whether that partner actually incurred the debt. The Limited Partnership has a General Partner and Limited Partners. Only a General Partner has authority to conduct partnership business and only a General Partner is liable for company debts. A Limited Partner has no control over the management of the company and has no personal liability for company debts (15 Pa.C.S.A. 8523, 8533).

But even a General Partner can avoid personal liability by forming a corporation, and then letting the corporation serve as the sole General Partner. An unpaid creditor of the Limited Partnership can sue the corporate General Partner, but not the shareholders of the corporation. Liability can be limited to the amount of money invested in the business venture. None of the owners will have personal liability. Of course, as with the corporation, all parties can be held personally liable for fraudulent or criminal acts performed in their partnership capacity.

The astute reader might be wondering "Why would anyone form a corporation (and pay all of the costs to set up the corporation) and then make the corporation the General Partner of a Limited Partnership (after having paid all that money to set up the Partnership)? If limited business liability is the goal, why not just form a corporation?"

The answers to that question are many and in fact, far removed from the original goal of limiting the business risk of the partners to just the money they invested in the business. The Limited Partnership can be used as a means of transferring a family business to the children with some significant tax benefits. For example, suppose Mom & Pop run a small, highly profitable, rapidly expanding, gourmet chocolate shop. They have two children, both in college. Right now, the business is worth about $500,000, but they figure that by the time they retire, the business could be worth millions. If their children inherit the business at that time, there could be significant Estate Taxes due. Also, because they are making lots of money right now, they are paying very high income taxes.

Both problems can be solved with a Family Limited Partnership. Mom and Pop can be the General Partners of the company and retain total control. They could make each child a Limited Partner by transferring 2% of the company to each child. This gift is worth less than the current annual Gift Tax Exclusion of $11,000, so the gift has no gift tax consequences. Mom and Pop can continue to gift shares of the partnership each year. By gifting a percentage of the business each year, the parents can essentially transfer all of the business to the children. When the parents die, there will be no Inheritance, Gift or Estate tax to be paid because the children already own the business. Of course there is still the problem of the Capital Gains tax should the children decide to sell the business.

Regardless of how much of the company they give away, Mom and Pop can keep total control of the company because they are the general partners. When the parents are ready to retire, one or both of the children can take over as General Partner — but if making chocolate is not their thing, the parents can arrange to have a corporation manage the Limited Partnership and the children continue to receive income as limited partners. As for the current income tax problem, the children, as limited partners, are entitled to receive income from the business. Income paid to the children and their parents is generally taxed at a lower rate than the taxes to just Mom and Pop. For example, suppose the company earns $100,000. Mom and Pop will pay a high rate of income tax if they are the only two partners in the company. If the children become partners, then each partner can earn $25,000 and the overall bill for income taxes will be smaller.

Still another important advantage of the Family Limited Partnership over the corporation is creditor protection for the children's partnership interest. For example, suppose one of the children, becomes a dentist, gets sued for malpractice, and loses the case. If Mom and Pop had incorporated the business and given the children most of the shares of stock in the company, the creditor could take the shares to satisfy the judgment. The creditor could wind up owning the company! Not so, with a Limited Partnership interest. A judge could order that the income from the Limited Partnership be used to pay the judgment, but he could not order the Partnership share itself to be given to the creditor unless the Limited Partnership Agreement allows for such transfer, or all other partners agree (15 Pa.C.S.A 8564).

Not likely with Mom and Pop as General Partners. They might even decide to pay the income to themselves and not distribute anything to the hapless creditor!

We used an actual business as an example to explain how the Limited Partnership worked. It didn't take Estate Planning attorneys long to figure out that the "family business" could be just income producing items (such as stocks and bonds) that Mom and Pop placed into the Limited Partnership. The family "business" could be just the business of earning income. In other words, the Family Limited Partnership (or even a Family Partnership) could just be a type of an Estate Plan created solely for the purpose of transferring assets to the children to avoid paying Estate Taxes, and to pay less in income taxes.

It didn't take the IRS long to challenge this method of Estate Planning. A series of IRS rulings and court cases followed, with the main issue being whether a bonafide business partnership existed.

There is a common sense rule of evidence that says "If it looks like a duck and walks like a duck, and quacks like a duck, it must be a duck." In 1946 the Supreme Court decided that whether a family partnership is really a business partnership for tax purposes, should be determined on a case by case basis; and that the IRS should use the "walk and quack" test. Only the justices said this in proper legal terms. They said to determine whether a partnership exists depends on ". . .whether the partners really and truly intended to join together for the purpose of carrying on a business and sharing in the profits or losses or both. And their intention in this respect is a question of fact, to be determined from testimony disclosed by their agreement, considered as a whole, and by their conduct in execution of its provisions" (*Commissioner v. Tower*, 327 U.S. 280 (1946)).

THE LIMITED LIABILITY COMPANY

The IRS continues to take a close look at family partnerships, and will challenge any tax break if the family partnership (limited or not) does not meet the basic requirement of being a bonafide business partnership. Perhaps in response to IRS challenges, in the 1990s each of the 50 states, and even the District of Columbia, passed laws enabling the residents of their state to form a new business entity called a **Limited Liability Company** ("LLC").

A Pennsylvania LLC is formed by filing a Certificate of Organization with the Pennsylvania Department of State. This new entity is not required to be a profit making venture. In Pennsylvania it can be formed for "...any lawful business except banking and insurance" (15 Pa.C.S.A. 8911, 15 Pa.C.S.A. 8914).

The LLC combines the better features of the Limited Partnership and the Corporation. Like the corporation, it can be formed by a single person who sets the rules of the company when he forms the corporation. The set of rules is called an **Operating Agreement**. The LLC can be run by a manager who is not a member of the company, or it can be run by a member or members of the company. As with a corporation, all members have limited liability, regardless of whether that member happens to be managing the company. As with a Limited Partnership, a creditor cannot take possession or control of a share of the company owned by a member unless the transfer is allowed by the Operating Agreement or all of the members agree to him becoming a member. In the absence of these, the most the creditor can do is get a court to assign income generated by that share to the creditor (15 Pa.C.S.A. 8922, 15 Pa.C.S.A 8924, 15 Pa.C.S.A. 8941).

Now Mom and Pop can form a LLC, give away some or all of the shares of the company during their lifetime, and still keep control of the company, and with no more personal liability than a non-managing member of the Limited Liability Company.

Transfers into the Limited Liability Company can be made so that there is no Estate or Gift tax issue. Income can be distributed to the children, or not, as Mom and Pop see fit.

The astute reader is probably thinking "Maximum control, limited liability, easily transferred to my heirs, no Estate tax. This is too good to be true. There must be a catch somewhere."

And so there is. It's called the Capital Gains tax. If you transfer property during your lifetime, that property is valued by the IRS as of the date of transfer. If you gift a share of the partnership during your lifetime, your beneficiary will take your basis in the property (i.e., the value that you paid for the partnership interest). If you sell the share to your beneficiary, then his basis is the fair market value of the share as of the date of purchase. Either way, once the beneficiary decides to sell the property, there may be a significant Capital Gains tax due.

An experienced Estate Planning attorney should be able to suggest any number of ways to solve the problem, including purchasing life insurance to pay the tax.

INSURANCE TO PAY DEBTS AND TAXES

Regardless of what form of business ownership you have, you need to think about what will happen to your business in the event of your incapacity or death. And in particular, how company debts will be paid. If your business is highly leveraged (business talk for "owes lots of money"), you also need to consider how those loans will be paid should you become disabled or die. One solution is to purchase Key man insurance. As explained earlier, Key man insurance is protection for the company against the loss of a valuable employee. The company purchases the policy and the proceeds are paid to the company to compensate it for the loss; but ultimately the policy benefits those who inherit the business.

Taxes are still another concern. Your business may be worth millions on paper, and your Estate Taxes will be based on that value. Your heirs might be forced to sell the company just to pay the taxes, but without your leadership they may get only a fraction of the value of the company.

Even if the federal government decides to eliminate federal Estate Taxes, the state of Pennsylvania, or any other state where you have a business location, may decide to levy an Estate or Inheritance tax.

And there is still the problem of the Capital Gains tax. No one in Congress is talking about doing away with the Capital Gains tax — and that tax could be sizeable. One solution to the problem of an unknown Estate Tax and/or Capital Gains tax is to purchase life insurance that can be used to pay for any Estate or Capital Gains taxes that may be due upon your death.

That may sound like a good simple solution, but you need to think things through before calling your insurance agent. The first question being:

How much insurance should I purchase?
That is a tough question. If you are in good health, who knows what will happen before you die. Will your business increase in value or go bust? Will the federal government really do away with Estate Taxes or will they do nothing and allow the tax to be reinstated in 2011?

The last question is particularly troublesome. Under today's tax law, if you purchase a life insurance policy, or even control the benefits of the policy, all of the proceeds of the policy will be counted as part of your taxable Estate. You may be buying insurance just to pay more in taxes to Uncle Sam.

You don't need a soothsayer or psychic to solve the problem. A financial planner with access to computer generated models can predict your life expectancy, how much your business will be worth when you retire and even the probability that the economy will require Estate taxes to be reinstated!

Suppose your financial planner predicts that Estate taxes will be reinstated and that your heirs will probably need to pay 1 million dollars. If you purchase a million dollar insurance policy, the value of the policy will be included in your Estate. If there is an Estate Tax of 40% your heirs will net only $600,000 of your million dollar policy, the rest going for Estate taxes on the proceeds of the policy itself.

Your heirs will need to come up with an additional $400,000 to make up for the original million dollars predicted as being necessary to pay your Estate taxes. The solution to this dilemma is the *Irrevocable Insurance Trust*.

THE IRREVOCABLE INSURANCE TRUST

An Irrevocable Insurance Trust can be designed to provide money to pay any tax that may be due after your death. To be sure that the IRS does not count the proceeds of the Trust as part of your taxable Estate the Trust must meet the following requirements:

⇨ The Trust must be irrevocable.

⇨ Neither you nor your spouse can be Trustee.

The Trust can be set up for the benefit of your child. In such case, the child can be Trustee of the Trust. The child, as Trustee, will purchase an insurance policy on your life. If you give the child a large sum of money to purchase the policy, then you may need to file a Gift Tax return. It is better to give the child $11,000 a year and have the child purchase a policy that is paid with quarterly or annual premiums instead of a single lump sum payment. If you are married, you and your spouse can gift up to $22,000 per year without the need to file a Gift Tax return.

As tax laws change, the child/Trustee can use as much of the gift as is needed to purchase sufficient insurance to cover the taxes. The Trust can be set up to cover Estate taxes or Capital Gains taxes, or both. For example, the Trustee can purchase an insurance policy that pays a million dollars upon your death. Those insurance funds can be used to pay your Estate taxes. Should it happen that no Estate taxes are due, the Trustee can keep the monies invested until the business is sold, when the Trust funds can be used to pay any Capital Gains tax that may be due. If monies are left over once all taxes are paid, they can be distributed to the named beneficiaries of the Trust.

Your attorney can design an Irrevocable Insurance Trust in any number of ways to meet the special needs of you and your family. For example, an Irrevocable Insurance Trust can be set up to solve problems described in the last Chapter. Alan wanted to leave insurance proceeds for his child but was concerned that the cash value of the policy could be taken by his creditors. A properly drafted Irrevocable Insurance Trust can solve such problem, because the Trust, and not Alan, is the owner of the policy.

Of course, it costs significant money to set up and maintain an Irrevocable Insurance Trust. Those who do not have concerns about creditors may wonder whether it's necessary to go through all that cost and bother if there will be no more Estate taxes in the future. After all a simple life insurance policy can cover any Capital Gains tax that may be due. But, as explained, the tax law as passed in 2001 reinstates the Estate Tax in 2011. If lawmakers take no further action, the Estate of anyone who dies on January 1, 2011, and thereafter is subject to an Estate Tax for an Estate over one million dollars.

Someone with an active imagination could envision the following scenario:

It is New Year's eve, 2010. A 97 year old lies sleeping, at his home, surrounded by his four grandchildren who are his sole heirs.

"He looks so peaceful."

"Yes. Surprising, considering that he has terminal cancer, failing kidneys and heart. His doctor says he can't last more than a few days. The doctor left a supply of morphine so that we can keep Gramps comfortable over the New Year's holiday. The doctor gave him a shot just before he left."

"The doctor said not to give Gramps another shot unless he was in pain. His heart is in such a weakened condition, he could easily overdose on morphine."

"Yes, of course."

"Too bad he didn't get a chance to do some Estate Planning before he had that stroke last year. "

"I thought his attorney took care of all that."

"His attorney suggested he set up an Irrevocable Insurance Trust to pay for any Estate Tax, but Gramps felt sure that Congress would pass a law that would permanently repeal the Estate Tax."

"I can't imagine Gramps coming to that conclusion. The economy is down and the government needs to raise taxes. It is easier for legislators to leave the law as written back in 2001, than take some affirmative action."

"Gramps was always an astute business man, but in his later years his mind wasn't as sharp as when he earned his 5 million dollars."

"Is that what we are going to inherit?"

"Not unless he dies before midnight. After midnight the Estate Tax is reinstated, and at a rate of 45%. Between state and federal taxes, we'll be lucky to come away with half a mill each."

"Gramps moved. I think he may be in pain."

"Yes, he does look uncomfortable."

"It isn't right to let him suffer like this."

"Yes, of course."

Continuing To Care 7

There are any number of reasons that people give for wanting to continue on with their lives. For the lucky ones, their main reason for living is that they are having a great time and don't want it to end. For many, it is more a sense of responsibility. During child rearing years the concern of the parent is what will happen to the child should the parent suddenly die. Once a child is grown, the roles often reverse, and it is the child worrying about what will happen to his parent if the child were not present to see to the care of the aging parent. Even pet lovers worry about what will happen to their pet should the owner no longer be around.

There is little that can be done to prepare those who depend on you for the loss of your companionship and emotional support; but there are many things you can do to provide financial support for those who rely on you. Even people of modest means can make financial provision so their loved ones will have an easy transition from being dependent to becoming self sufficient.

This chapter explains the many simple, and relatively inexpensive, things you can do to provide care for your loved ones should you not be present to do so yourself.

CARING FOR THE MINOR CHILD

It doesn't happen very often, but both parents could die or become incapacitated before their child reaches adulthood. Most parents don't want to think about, much less prepare for such a happening. But in this age of postponing parenthood, many parents are raising children into their fifties and sixties. The probability of a life threatening illness increases with age, so parents need to understand the importance of planning ahead.

Parents with dangerous occupations also need to provide for the care of their minor child in event of the disability or death of both parents. It is surprising to think of how many of us are employed in dangerous occupations. Construction workers, military personnel, firemen, state and federal law enforcement agents, and in this day and age, even postal workers face hazards on a daily basis.

Regardless of the parent's age or occupation, planning for the care of a minor child should be part of every parent's Estate Plan, not only because it is the responsible thing to do, but also because it is relatively simple and inexpensive to do.

A child must be cared for in two ways, the **person** of the child and the **property** of the child. To care for the person of the child, someone must be in charge of the child's everyday living, not only food and shelter but to provide social, ethical and religious training. Someone must have legal authority to make medical decisions and see to the child's education. To care for the child's property, someone must be responsible to see that monies left to the child are used for the care of the child and that anything left over is preserved until the child becomes an adult.

A Guardian will need to be appointed to care for the person and property of the child in the event that both parents become incapacitated or die before the child is grown.

USING A WILL TO APPOINT A GUARDIAN

As explained in Chapter 4, each parent can use his/her Will to appoint someone to serve as Guardian of their minor child in the event that both parents die before the child is grown.

It is a good idea for both parents to name the same person to serve as Guardian. If the parents appoint different people for the job and then die simultaneously, it will be up to the Judge to decide who is best suited to be Guardian. If they do not die simultaneously, then the Court will give top priority to the person named in the Will of the last parent to die (20 Pa.C.S.A.2519).

One problem with using a Will to appoint someone to be your child's Guardian, is that for the appointment to be effective, the Will must be admitted to Probate; i.e., the Court must determine that the Will is valid; and the person you chose as Guardian needs to file a petition to be appointed as the child's Guardian. It might take several weeks before that person has the legal authority to care for the child. A better solution is to appoint someone as a *Standby Guardian* who can immediately assume responsibility for the care of the minor child, should the need arise.

APPOINTING A STANDBY GUARDIAN

Appointing a Standby Guardian is easily done by signing the statutory form of the DESIGNATION OF STANDBY GUARDIAN (23 Pa.C.S.A. 5611). The form can be copied at any law library or downloaded from Internet. See page vii for the Web site address.

The DESIGNATION needs to be signed by the parent who has custody of the child. If both parents are caring for the child, then they both need to sign the Designation in the presence of two witnesses. The Designation gives the Standby Guardian the right to care for the child for sixty days following the *Triggering Event* named by the parent in the Designation. Parents usually define the Triggering Event as the death or incapacity of the custodial parent.

The Standby Guardian needs to sign the DESIGNATION indicating that he/she agrees to care for the child should the Triggering Event happens.

Once the Standby Guardian is notified that the Triggering Event has taken place, he/she can immediately take over the care of the child. Within 60 days of the Triggering Event, the Standby Guardian needs to petition the Court to be appointed as the legal Guardian of the minor if the parent is deceased; or to serve as Co-guardian with the parent if the parent is incapacitated. If the Standby Guardian does not apply to be appointed as Guardian within the 60 days, the Standby Guardianship terminates and the Court may appoint someone else to serve as the Guardian of the person of the child. If the child is left with significant property, the Court will probably appoint a Guardian for the property of the child as well.

Considering how simple it is to appoint a Standby Guardian, even healthy parents should consider doing so. The appointment of Standby Guardian becomes effective only upon the Triggering Event; so appointing a Standby Guardian does not change the right of the parent to care for the child. The parent is free to revoke the Designation at any time during his lifetime, should circumstances change. This can be done by destroying the **DESIGNATION OF STANDBY GUARDIAN** and notifying the Standby Guardian that the document has been revoked (23 Pa.C.S.A. 5603, 23 Pa.C.S.A. 5614).

COURT APPROVAL OF STANDBY GUARDIAN

The single parent who is seriously ill, or the single parent who is in the armed forces may want to have his attorney file a petition in the Court to approve his Designation of Standby Guardian. The benefit of having Court approval of the Standby Guardian is that should the Triggering Event happen, the Standby Guardian can take over the care of the minor without the need for any further confirmation by the Court (23 Pa.C.S.A. 5613).

THE BEST CHOICE OF GUARDIAN

Many parents never get around to appointing a Guardian because they cannot come to an agreement as to the best choice of Guardian. "I think my mother should be Guardian. After all she raised me, and I turned out fine." can signal the opening salvo of a lengthy, and often unresolved battle.

Not being able to agree on a choice of Guardian should not discourage you from appointing the person of your choice either as part of your Will or in a separate writing. The thing to keep in mind is that the Guardian of your choice will take over only if the other parent is deceased or incapacitated. Even if you both die simultaneously, and you each name someone different to serve as Guardian, your choice of Guardian will at least be brought to the attention of the Court.

When making your appointment, the thing to keep in mind is what is best for the child. It is important that the Guardian be compatible with the child, because in the Commonwealth of Pennsylvania, a child who is 14 or older can express his preference to the Judge. The Judge will give that person priority unless the Court finds that it is not in the child's best interest to appoint the child's choice of Guardian.

The Court will also consider, and where appropriate give priority, to a person who is of the same religion as the parents of the minor child (20 Pa.C.S.A. 5113).

LEAVING PROPERTY FOR THE CHILD

As any parent is well aware, it is expensive to raise a child. The person you consider to be the best choice to serve as Guardian might not be able to do so unless you leave sufficient monies to pay for the care of the child. If you have limited finances, consider purchasing a term life insurance policy on your life and/or on the life of the other parent of the child. If you can only afford one policy, insure the life of the parent who contributes most to the support of the child.

Term insurance policies are relatively inexpensive if you limit the term to just that period of time until your child becomes an adult. Some companies offer a combination of term life and disability insurance, in the event that the bread-winner becomes disabled and unable to work. As with any other purchase, it is important to comparison shop to obtain the best price for the coverage.

If you are married, you may want to name your spouse as the beneficiary of the term insurance policy with your child as an alternate beneficiary. Married or single, you can name your child as the primary beneficiary of the policy. The insurance company may give amounts up to $10,000 to whoever has custody of the child. The company is required to seek Court permission to transfer funds to a minor that exceed $10,000 (20 Pa.C.S.A 5307).

If the insurance funds are no more than $25,000, the Court may decide to have the funds transferred directly to the child or to whoever is caring for the child. The Court can order that the child's funds be deposited in a bank until the child is 18. But for significant sums of money he will probably require that a Guardian be appointed to care for the property of the child (20 Pa.C.S.A. 5101, 20 Pa.C.S.A. 5103).

CONTINUING TO CARE

AVOIDING AN UNNECESSARY GUARDIANSHIP

We discussed the ways parents can control who is appointed to serve as the Guardian of their minor child should both parents be incapacitated or deceased. Guardianship is a necessity in such cases. But if at least one of the parents is able to care for the person of the child, it may be wise to avoid the need for the Court to appoint a Guardian of the property. If you leave the child a significant amount of money the Court will appoint a Guardian of that property. Even if the surviving parent is appointed to serve as Guardian, the amount you leave to the child will be reduced by the cost of establishing and maintaining the guardianship.

An attorney must be employed to establish the guardianship. Once appointed, the Guardian has many duties. He must prepare an inventory and the Court may require an annual accounting for monies spent (20 Pa.C.S.A 5142, 20 Pa.C.S.A. 5161). The Guardian is entitled to be paid for his services. He may need to employ an accountant to assist with the preparation of the inventory and accounting. Court filing fees, Guardian and attorney fees, accounting fees, are all proper charges to the child's guardianship property.

Monies left for the care of the child may be significantly reduced by the cost of caring for the property. This can be avoided by leaving property to the child in such a manner, that will make it unnecessary for the Court to appoint a Guardian of the property of the child. One way to do so is to set up a Trust for the child, but if you have limited finances, then a good alternative is to appoint someone to serve as Custodian of the gift under the *Pennsylvania Uniform Transfers to Minors Act*.

THE UNIFORM TRANSFERS TO MINORS ACT

The Pennsylvania Uniform Transfers to Minors Act is designed to protect gifts made to a minor by appointing someone to be the *Custodian* of a gift until the child is grown. For example, you can make a minor child the beneficiary of your life insurance policy, by naming a trusted relative or friend or even a financial institution to be the Custodian of the gift. Should you die while the child is a minor, the insurance company will give the proceeds of the policy to the person you named as Custodian to hold until the child is 21.

If you wish to make a gift to a minor in your Will. You can appoint your Personal Representative (or anyone else) to be the Custodian of the gift until the child reaches the age specified in your Will. For example: "I give the sum of $20,000 to _____ (name) as custodian for _____ (name of minor) until the age of _____under the Pennsylvania Uniform Transfers to Minors Act."

Under Pennsylvania law, the gift must be distributed at age 21, however you can extend that up to age 25 by filling in the age as indicated above (20 Pa.C.S.A. 5321).

You can even use the Pennsylvania Uniform Transfers to Minors Law to make a gift during your lifetime of some item such as shares in a corporation or a limited partnership interest. You can nominate yourself as Custodian of the gift, or you can name another person to serve as Custodian. Once the lifetime gift is made it becomes irrevocable, so this method is not appropriate unless you are sure that you want the child to have the gift once he/she is of age (20 Pa.C.S.A 5304, 20 Pa.C.S.A. 5309, 20 Pa.C.S.A 5311).

THE CUSTODIAN'S DUTIES

While the Custodian is in possession of the gift, he can use as much of the gift as he thinks advisable for the benefit of the child. He can pay monies directly to the child, or use the funds for the child's benefit. In making the distribution he is not obliged to take into account that someone else has a duty to support the child — even if the Custodian is the child's parent and it is his own responsibility to support the child (20 Pa.C.S.A. 5314).

The Custodian can do the opposite and distribute nothing. He can refuse to use any of the monies for the child and just keep the funds invested until the child is 21. In such case, the child's parent or guardian (or even the child once he is 14) can ask a Court to order that the monies be used for the care of the child. The Judge will determine what is in the child's best interest and then rule on the matter.

Hopefully, the Custodian will give a regular accounting to the child's parent or guardian. If not, any member of the child's family, or the child once he/she reaches 14, can ask the Court to order a full accounting of the custodial property (20 Pa.C.S.A. 5319).

As with any type of Estate Plan, you need to examine all aspects of the transfer to see if there is anything that may be objectionable to you.

THE CUSTODIAN'S FEE

The law requires the Custodian to invest and manage the property in a responsible, prudent manner. The Custodian is entitled to be paid for his effort. If the gift is sizeable, his fee can be sizeable. Before appointing a person or a financial institution as Custodian, it is best to come to a written agreement about how the property will be managed and the charge for doing so (20 Pa.C.S.A. 5315).

NO GROUP GIFT

You cannot make a gift to more than one child under the Uniform Transfers To Minors Act. For example, if you want to make a single gift of real property to two or more minor children, you need to do so by another method, such as creating a Trust for the children (20 Pa.C.S.A. 5310).

THE COST OF PROBATE

As discussed, you can include a gift to a minor in your Will by naming a Custodian for the gift. But as with any gift made under a Will, a Probate procedure will be necessary to distribute the gift to the Custodian, or to the child if he is of age. If you are trying to avoid Probate, then this may not be the best way to go. For sizeable gifts, the better route is to set up a Revocable Living Trust. You can manage the Trust while you are able. Should you become incapacitated or die before the child is grown your Successor Trustee will take over.

You can instruct the Successor Trustee to use his best discretion to either keep the funds invested until the child reaches a certain age; or to use as much of the funds as necessary to care for the child in the event that the child's parents are unable to do so. Which brings us to another problem, namely, that there is no flexibility as to the final distribution of a gift made under the Uniform Transfers to Minors Act.

MANDATORY DISTRIBUTION

A Custodian appointed under the Pennsylvania Uniform Transfers To Minors Act must distribute the gift when the child is 21 (or up to 25 if you so indicated). The gift must be made regardless of whether the child has sufficient maturity to handle the money in a responsible manner. A sizeable gift to an immature beneficiary is not the best Estate Plan.

PROVIDING FOR THE STEPCHILD

Perhaps the reason that the story of Cinderella has such universal appeal is that many stepchildren, at one point or another, feel left out. The law seems to reinforce that perception. Unless a married person makes provision otherwise, a spouse has priority over the child in health matters both before and after death. If a married person is too ill to make medical decisions, the doctors will turn to the spouse for directions. Should a married person die, the decedent's spouse and not the child, has the authority to agree to an autopsy or anatomical gift (20 Pa.C.S.A. 8611, 35 P.S. 1111). If a married couple holds all property jointly, that property will go to the surviving spouse and not to the child of the deceased parent. This might not be a problem if the surviving spouse is the natural parent of the child. It could be a major problem if the natural parent dies first. The stepchild of the surviving parent may be left with nothing.

In such situations, the stepparent comes across as villain, but it is the parent, and not the stepparent, who decides whether the child will inherit property belonging to the natural parent. Too often the stepchild is left out by default, i.e., the natural parent doesn't give the matter any thought, or perhaps the natural parent is confident that the stepparent will do "what's right."

That was the case with Walter. He always wanted to be a father, so he was pleased when Todd was born just before the first anniversary of Walter's marriage to Nancy. Twin girls were born just 15 months later. Unfortunately the twins' birth was premature, causing them to have medical and developmental problems. Nancy had her hands full just caring for the three children, so it was up to Walter to support the family.

Walter was up to the job. He was both conscientious and ambitious. He started his own interior decorating business, complete with a retail sales storefront to sell fabrics, and an upholstery shop in the rear of the store. With hard work and long hours, he was able to make a comfortable living. But the strain of raising a family and running a business took its toll, both on him and the marriage. At 40, he felt like an old man.

All that changed when he hired Annie to manage the retail part of his business. Her energy and sunny disposition were just what the business (and Walter) needed.

Walter's divorce from Nancy was amicable. Walter was a loving father who took his responsibilities seriously. He was generous when it came to supporting the children. Walter had only finished high school, and he wanted more for his son. He encouraged Todd to do well in school so that he could go on to college, and maybe become a doctor or lawyer. The twins had developmental problems; but Walter encouraged them to reach their maximum potential. It was his goal to help them become self sufficient.

Annie got along very well with her stepchildren. She had no trouble with Walter's desire to support the children and give them a good start in life. Even though they held all of their money in a joint account, she never questioned any expense made on behalf of the children.

Walter never gave much thought to an Estate Plan. After all, he was healthy, and in the prime of his earning capacity. He often said that he was fortunate to have married two wonderful women. If he had a dark thought, it soon passed, rationalizing that if something happened to him, Annie would take care of the children.

But she didn't.

Walter died in one of those freak accidents. He was trimming the branches from his tree with an electric saw and accidently touched an overhead wire. All he owned was tied up in the business that he held jointly with Annie. Annie felt that she was a major factor in the success of that business. Why should she share any of her hard earned money with Nancy? As for the children, it was Nancy's job to raise them. After all they were Nancy's children, and not Annie's children. If it was a struggle to support the children, then that was Nancy's problem!

A better argument (but one she didn't raise) was that Walter really wanted Annie to inherit everything. If he wanted to provide for his children, he could have done so in any number of different ways, beginning with his marriage to Annie:

- He could have insisted on a prenuptial agreement that would have provided for certain funds to be kept separate for the benefit of his children.

- He could have signed a partnership agreement with Annie that would have given his share of the business to his children, in the event of his death.

- If he didn't want to negotiate with Annie about a prenuptial agreement or a partnership agreement, he could have had his attorney prepare a Trust that would have cared for the children until they were old enough to be on their own.

- If nothing else, he could have purchased a life insurance policy with the children as beneficiaries of the policy.

THE SECOND MARRIAGE TRUST

Walter's situation is not unique. Second marriages are commonplace in America. Many who are widowed or divorced, remarry. If children are involved, the parent may have divided loyalties. The parent may want to provide income to the child until the child completes his education, and then leave whatever is left of his Estate to his surviving spouse. More often it is the other way around. The parent wants to be sure that the surviving spouse has sufficient income to support his/her current life-style, but once the surviving spouse dies, the parent wants all that remains to go to his children. A properly drafted Trust can provide for the care of a spouse and child in whatever way the Grantor of the Trust thinks best.

That was the case with an elderly widower who married a pretty girl less than half his age. Their prenuptial agreement made it clear that all his property would go to his son from his first marriage. Surprisingly, the marriage turned out well. So well that the couple had two daughters. The husband decided to divide his Estate equally between his three children and to provide for the care of his wife until the youngest child was grown.

His attorney suggested a Trust. "You can be Trustee during your lifetime. Once you die, your Successor Trustee can immediately distribute one-third of the Trust to your son who is now 55. No sense to keep him waiting. The rest of your money can remain in your Trust. Income from the Trust can be used to support your wife and children until the youngest is 25. Then, whatever remains in the Trust can be distributed equally to your daughters."

"Good idea" said the elderly gentlemen, with a smile "Just make sure it is revocable during my lifetime. Who knows what adventures I might be up to in the future?"

PROVIDING FOR THE ADULT CHILD

It isn't just stepchildren who can be left out if no provision is made. Even children from a long-standing marriage can be cut off against the wishes of a parent. A parent may assume that all of their children will be treated equally when both parents are gone, but if all their property is held jointly, the last parent to die is the one who gets to decide "who gets what." Too often, the wishes of the deceased parent are ignored, for example:

THE STRAINED RELATIONSHIP A child may have a close relationship with one parent, and a strained, but tolerable, relationship with the other. Peace in the family is achieved because the parent who is close to the child acts as a buffer. Should the buffer parent die first, the relationship between the surviving parent and the child may fall apart altogether and the child's inheritance be cut off.

THE PARENT WITH DIMINISHED CAPACITY The more common scenario, is that the surviving parent becomes increasingly dependent on one child — either for emotional support, or for physical assistance as the parent ages. The other children may live at a distance, or perhaps they are too involved with their own family to assist. The supporting child may end up with most, if not all, of what was intended for all of the children.

These problems can be avoided by having your attorney prepare a Family Trust. The family assets are placed in the Trust with the parents as co-Trustees. The beneficiaries of the Trust cannot be changed unless both parents agree to the change. Once one parent dies, the Trust becomes irrevocable. The Trust income goes to the surviving parent and once that parent dies, whatever remains in the Trust is distributed in the manner as was agreed by both parents.

CARING FOR THOSE WHO CAN'T

The caregiver of someone who is incapacitated, or developmentally disabled needs to, as part of his Estate Plan, provide for the care of the incapacitated person as well as himself. Should the caregiver become disabled or die, someone will need to take over and make medical decisions for the incapacitated person and see to it that he/she is properly housed and fed.

An aging parent of a developmentally disabled child may worry about how the child will manage without the parent to oversee his care. An aged spouse caring for his incapacitated spouse, may be concerned about who will care for the ill spouse should he die first. Often a family member will agree to take responsibility for the care of an incapacitated person; but perhaps no one wants the job.

If there are large sums of money involved it may be the opposite case, too many people may want to be in control. One family member may want the incapacitated child or spouse to remain at home with the assistance of a home health care worker. Another may think the best place is an assisted living facility with 24 hour care. The caregiver may be concerned that a tug-of-war will erupt once he dies.

In such case, the caregiver should consult with an attorney to ensure future care for the incapacitated person. The attorney may suggest that a guardianship be set up with the caregiver and his choice of successor caregiver serving as Co-Guardians. The Co-Guardian can take full responsibility for the job should the caregiver become disabled or die. Once the Guardianship is in place, the Court will continue to supervise the care of the incapacitated person until he/she is restored to capacity or dies (20 Pa.C.S.A. 5514).

The only problem with setting up a guardianship while the caregiver is able to care for the disabled spouse or child is the cost of the procedure. It may cost hundreds, if not thousands, of dollars to set up and maintain the guardianship. If the incapacitated person is without funds, the caregiver can ask Pennsylvania Legal Services for assistance. See page xii for information about finding the nearest Legal Services office.

Those who have adequate funds may hesitate to go through the effort and expense to set up a guardianship if it may be not be needed for years to come.

An alternative is for the caregiver to make provision in his Will for the appointment of a Guardian. Under Pennsylvania law, whoever makes a gift in his Will to a minor child or an incapacitated person, may appoint someone to serve as Guardian of property left to the incapacitated person (20 Pa.C.S.A. 5115, 20 Pa.C.S.A. 5121, 20 Pa.C.S.A. 5146, 20 Pa.C.S.A. 5514, 20 Pa.C.S.A. 5515).

If the gift is sizeable, the caregiver might decided to set up a Trust, either as part of his Will or included as part of his Inter Vivos Trust. Instead of a Court supervised guardianship, the person named as Trustee can care for the property of the incapacitated person. One problem with establishing a Trust for the incapacitated person is the possible loss of government benefits. To avoid that problem the attorney can draft a SPECIAL NEEDS TRUST.

A SPECIAL NEEDS TRUST FOR THE INCAPACITATED

Government assistance is available to provide medical and custodial care for those who are incapacitated and without the means to care for themselves. Both state and federal government provide such assistance with programs such as Social Security disability benefits and Medicaid. The family often supplements the government program by providing for the incapacitated person's *special needs* or *supplemental needs* such as clothing, hobbies, special education, outings to a movie or a sports event — things that give the incapacitated person some quality of life.

This is not a problem while family members are alive and able to provide for the incapacitated person. The worry is how to continue that care should the provider die. To be eligible for government assistance programs the incapacitated person must essentially be without funds. Family members fear that leaving money to the incapacitated in a Will or Trust will disqualify the incapacitated person from receiving government assistance. Understanding this dilemma, the federal government allows a parent, grandparent or legal guardian to set up a *Special Needs Trust* for persons under the age of 65, who are disabled as defined by 42 U.S.C. 1382c(a)(3).

A Trust set up in this manner makes an irrevocable gift to the incapacitated person — only the gift is held in Trust. The federal statute allows the Trustee to use Trust funds to provide for the special needs of the incapacitated; provided that whatever funds remain in the Trust after the incapacitated person dies, are used to reimburse the state for monies spent on his behalf (42 U.S.C. 1396p(d)(4)(A)).

This may present a problem to the parent who wants to set up the Trust. If he gives too little, the funds may not last for the lifetime of the incapacitated person. If he gives too much, then there may be a sizeable "donation" to the state as repayment for government benefits provided to the incapacitated person.

Parents of a disabled child may decide to solve the problem, by leaving money to another family member with verbal instructions to take care of the child's special needs once the parents are deceased. Of course the problem with that approach, is that once the funds are left to the family member, they become his property and available to his creditors. A *Discretionary Trust*, may be a better solution.

A Discretionary Trust differs from the Medicaid Special Needs Trust in that monies placed in the Trust do not represent a gift to the incapacitated person. The Trustee can use Trust funds for the benefit of the incapacitated person, or not, as the Trustee sees fit. The incapacitated person owns none of the Trust property, so money left in the Trust when the incapacitated person dies can be distributed to other beneficiaries of the Trust.

Pennsylvania Courts have ruled that a Discretionary Trust will not be considered as the property of the person receiving public Medical Assistance, provided the Trustee has the power to distribute property and income to more than one beneficiary (*Lang v. Commonwealth of Pa.*, Dept. of Public Welfare, 598 A.2d 1283 (Pa. 1987); *Snyder v. Commonwealth of Pa.*, Dept. of Public Welfare, 598 A.2d 1283 (Pa. 1991)). There are other technical Trust provisions that need to be included in the Trust in order for it to qualify as a Discretionary Trust; so is important that an experienced Elder Law attorney prepare the document.

CARING FOR YOUR PET

*A woman died at peace,
leaving her fortune
and care of her cat to her niece.
Alas, the fortune and the cat
Soon disappeared after that.*

You could leave money to someone with the understanding that the person will take care of your pet, but the moral of the above limerick, is that just leaving money will not guarantee care for your pet. The better route is to have your attorney prepare a Will that includes specific instructions and funds to provide for the care of your pet during its lifetime. Those with a Revocable Living Trust can include a similar provision as part of the Trust. The provision for your pet should include directions for how the remaining funds are to be distributed after the death of the pet.

A TRUST TO CARE FOR YOUR PET

If you are financially able and have several pets, you may want to set up a special Trust for the care of your pets. The person you name as Trustee will be charged with the duty to use Trust funds to pay for the care of those animals who survive you. You also need to name a residuary beneficiary (a person or perhaps a charitable organization) to receive whatever remains in the Trust once all of the animals are deceased. Animal support groups, such as the Humane Society, have people who will care for the pet of a deceased owner. You might consider appointing such group as the remainder beneficiary of the Trust in exchange for the lifetime care of your pet(s).

If you don't have the resources to set up a Trust to care for your pet, you can still ask a fellow pet lover to care for the animal. If no one among your circle of family and friends is able to do so, then ask your pet's veterinarian to consider starting an "Orphaned Pet Service" to assist in finding new homes for pets who lose their owners. It is good public relations and a potential source of income. If this is agreeable to the Veterinarian, you can make arrangements in your Will to pay the Vet to care for the pet until a suitable family can be found. This is a more humane approach than the, all too common practice, of putting a pet "to sleep" rather than have the pet suffer the loss of its master. And in at least one case, that reasoning backfired.

Eleanor always had a pet in the house. After her husband died, her two poodles were her constant companions. When Eleanor became ill with cancer, she worried about what would happen to her "buddies" without her to care for them. She finally decided it best to have her family put them to sleep when she died.

Eleanor endured surgery, chemotherapy, radiation therapy, and even some holistic remedies, but she continued to go downhill. Eleanor's family came in to visit her at the hospital to say their last good-byes. She was so ill, she didn't even recognize them. No one thought she could last the day. Because the family was from out of state, and time short, they decided to put the pets to sleep so they need only take care of the funeral arrangements when she died.

To everyone's surprise, Eleanor rallied. She lived two more long, lonely years.

She often said she wished they had put her to sleep instead of her buddies.

THE CHARITABLE TRUST

We explained how a Trust can be set up to care for a pet and whatever is left over (the remainder) given to a charitable organization. There are other kinds of charitable trusts that can be set up to benefit the giver as well as the receiver. For example, suppose you own stock which has appreciated substantially over the years, but pays few dividends. This hasn't been a problem in the past because you earned a good income. But now you wish to retire, and will need additional income. You would like to cash in the stock and invest the funds in something that can supplement your retirement income, but your accountant says that a significant portion of the value of the stock will go to Uncle Sam as payment for the Capital Gains Tax.

By now you know that a clever Estate Planning attorney will have any number of ways to solve the problem. The dialogue with your attorney might go something like this:

ATTORNEY: "Do you have a favorite charity?"

"Yes, why do you ask?"

ATTORNEY: "You can set up a Charitable Remainder Trust and donate the stock to that charity by depositing the stock in the Trust. Charities don't pay taxes, so the stock can be sold and the proceeds invested in property that produces a good income. In return for the donation, you can receive an income for the next 20 years or you can receive a monthly annuity based on your life expectancy."

"What's in it for the charity?"

ATTORNEY: "The charity gets whatever is left after paying you the annuity."

"Yes, but suppose I die next year, and my wife is left without the securities and no income."

ATTORNEY: "No problem. If you decide on a 20 year annuity, you can name your wife or any other beneficiary to receive the balance of the annuity. If you wish, you can have an annuity based on your life expectancy and that of your spouse. If you predecease your spouse, then the income continues until she dies."

"It seems to me that if the annuity is based on my life expectancy <u>AND</u> my wife's life expectancy, there won't be much left for the charity."

ATTORNEY: "How much is left for the charity depends on the value of the gift and the cost of the annuity. The cost of the annuity depends on the combined life expectancy of you and your wife. I think the best way to understand this plan is for you to look at actual numbers. There are any number of ways to set up a Charitable Remainder Trust. I can explain each option to you. For each option, I will give you the cost of setting up the program; the amount of money you will get; and how much money will actually go to your favorite charity. Of course it must be an IRS approved charity (IRC 501(c)(3))."

Once you see the numbers you can make an informed decision as to whether you want to sell the stock and pay the Capital Gains Tax, or set up a Charitable Trust and receive an income."

"Good idea."

THE FUTURE OF ESTATE PLANNING

Up till now Estate Planning for the wealthy was all about the Estate Tax. Estate Planning attorneys would spend their time dreaming up different ways to reduce Estate taxes for their wealthy clients. The IRS would spend their time examining and challenging any Estate plan that appeared too innovative. It seems likely that by 2010 the Estate Tax will be a memory. Is the game over?

Hardly. As explained in Chapter 3, instead of paying an Estate Tax, the child who inherits property that has appreciated more than 1.3 million dollars will pay a substantial Capital Gains Tax when he sells the property. In a way, that makes sense. A major criticism of the Estate Tax was that the tax had to be paid within 9 months of the date of death. That created a hardship for those inheriting a small business with a high assessed value but with no cash to pay taxes on that value.

Critics of the Estate Tax often cited the example of the cash poor farm located on valuable land. Once the owner of the farm died, the family would be forced to sell the farm just to pay Estate Taxes. By substituting the Capital Gains tax for the Estate Tax, that problem is eliminated. No Capital Gains Tax need be paid until the beneficiary decides to sell the property. Theoretically, the family farm can now be inherited generation to generation with no tax consequence.

But there are few family farms in today's economy. Future heirs are more likely to inherit highly appreciated real property or securities that they will eventually want to sell. And when they do, they may need to pay a significant Capital Gains tax. In Pennsylvania Capital Gains is taxed as ordinary income; so the resident of Pennsylvania will pay taxes on the Capital Gain to the federal government and to the state of Pennsylvania, as well (72 P.S. 7301).

More than likely any Capital Gains tax levied as a result of inheriting property with a low basis, will have its counterpart in state taxes. The new game for Estate Planning attorneys will be to devise an Estate Plan that will reduce the Capital Gains Tax. The IRS and the Pennsylvania Department of Revenue will, no doubt, enjoy challenging those plans. One tried (and legal) method of reducing the Capital Gains Tax is the Charitable Remainder Trust as was just discussed. It doesn't take a crystal ball to see that this could well be the basis of future Estate Plans, so we will take a few more pages to describe the pros and cons of the Trust.

THE CHARITABLE REMAINDER ANNUITY TRUST

A **Charitable Remainder Annuity Trust** is a Trust that is established according to the Internal Revenue Code (IRC 664). Charities do not pay taxes, so property donated to the Trust can be sold by the Trustee free of the Capital Gains Tax. Money from the sale is invested so that it provides an income (an *annuity*) to the beneficiary (the *annuitant*) for a fixed period of time, say 20 years, or for the annuitant's lifetime as computed by actuarial tables (i.e., life expectancy tables). The charity receives whatever is left (the *remainder*) after payment of the annuity. How much income the donor will receive and how much the charity will receive, is agreed upon at the time the Trust is set up.

The Trust can be set up in any number of ways depending on the goal of the **donor** (the person making the gift). In the example just given, the goal of the donor was to convert non-income producing property to income producing property without paying a high Capital Gains Tax. A wealthy donor may be more concerned about his child paying a high Capital Gains Tax should the child inherit highly appreciated property.

For example, suppose you bought acreage in western Pennsylvania that appreciated significantly over the years and is now worth 1 million dollars. You have been putting off selling the property because of the Capital Gains Tax. But it has been a burden to you. It produces no income and because the property continues to appreciate, each year you pay more and more in property taxes. You did not mind the sacrifice because you figured that your son would inherit the property at a step-up in basis. But now with the new tax law, by the time you die, the property may be worth 2 million dollars. He is only allowed a 1.3 million dollar step up in basis, so your son may need to pay a significant Capital Gains Tax when he sells the property.

Setting up a Charitable Remainder Annuity Trust solves the problem of the Capital Gains Tax. The land is transferred to the Charitable Trust. Charities pay no tax, so the Trustee can sell the land and the full market value of the property will be available for investment.

The Trust could be set up with you receiving an income for life, and your son receiving the annuity after your death. The only problem with this arrangement is that your son is significantly younger than you are. There may not be much left to benefit the charity if they must wait for both of you to die. The solution is to have the annuity based on your life only and then use part of the income that you receive to purchase a 2 million dollar insurance policy on your life with your son as beneficiary. The 2 million dollars is the estimated value of the land that your son would have inherited at your death. But with this arrangement he will inherit the insurance proceeds free of any Capital Gains Tax.

The astute reader (and probably one with an accounting background) will say "Aha, you may have avoided the Capital Gains Tax, but the Estate Tax Exclusion value does not increase to 2 million dollars until the year 2006. The 2 million dollar life insurance policy counts as part of your taxable Estate, so if you die before 2006, your son will pay an Estate Tax! "

And of course our imaginary Clever Attorney has a solution in the form of an Irrevocable Insurance Trust. You can set up an Irrevocable Trust so that the Trust owns the insurance policy and not you. The insurance policy is not included in your taxable Estate, so your son pays no Estate Tax. See page 96 for an explanation of how the Irrevocable Insurance Trust works.

As with any Estate Plan you need to consider the downside, and the Charitable Remainder Annuity Trust is no exception.

☒   **ATTORNEY FEES**
It may cost significant attorney fees to set up the Trust. Some charities may offer to have their attorney prepare the Trust at no cost to you, or perhaps they offer a "standard" Trust document that their attorney prepared. But, using their Trust document represents a conflict of interest. Their Trust was prepared by an attorney for the greatest benefit to his client (that's the charity, not you). It is important that you employ your own attorney to represent you. He knows the extent of your Estate and he understands what you wish to accomplish.

☒ THE COMPLEXITY OF THE PLAN

A Charitable Remainder Annuity Trust is a sophisticated Estate Plan designed to benefit the well-to-do donor and an IRS approved charity. There are any number of ways to set up the plan. It is important to have an attorney who will take the time to explore different plans until you determine the best plan for you.

☒ THE TRUST IS IRREVOCABLE

Once established, the Trust is not revocable, so it is important that you understand all of the aspects of the Trust. In particular, you need to know how much it will cost in attorney's fees to set up the Trust; and how much income you will receive, and over what period of time. The income you receive as an annuitant is taxable to you. You need to consider that while taxes change over the years, the terms of the Trust cannot be changed. It is important that your attorney, accountant or financial planner give you some idea of what you might expect in terms of future income tax payments.

Although future income tax payments may be a question mark, the power of the Charitable Remainder Trust is the tax benefit to the donor at the time the Trust is set up.

☑ NO CAPITAL GAINS TAX

Had you sold the property and invested the money yourself, you would have had to pay a Capital Gains Tax and that tax could be substantial, depending on the tax rate in effect at the time of the transfer. By gifting the property the full value of the land can be used to produce investment income.

☑ NO PROPERTY TAX

Once your property is transferred into the Trust, you will no longer need to pay annual property taxes.

☑   **NO GIFT TAX**

The property you transfer into the Trust is a gift to a charity and as such is not included in the sum total of taxable gifts that you give during your lifetime.

☑   **INCOME TAX DEDUCTION**

Because you are making a charitable donation, you should be able to take a charitable deduction on your income tax in the year of the donation.

There are other "perks" in addition to tax benefits.

☑   **NO PROBATE EXPENSE**

It might take an expensive and time consuming Probate procedure to transfer the property to a beneficiary upon your death. By transferring the property to the Trust during your lifetime, you avoid the need for a Probate procedure to transfer the property after your death.

☑   **GIVE WHEN NEEDED INSTEAD OF LATER**

A Charitable Remainder Annuity Trust can be set up in any number of different ways to accommodate your Estate Plan. For example, if you are not in need of a present income, but expect that you will spend significant sums on your child's education, you can set up a 20 year annuity with your child as the annuitant. This will get the child through college and probably be a great help should the child decide to start a family. Why have the child inherit property in later, high earning years rather than in the early, high expense/low income years?

☑   CREDITOR PROTECTION

If you keep the land and are sued, you could lose it to pay your creditors. If a beneficiary inherits the land, it could be lost to his/her creditors. But once the property is transferred to the Trust, the gift is made. Neither your creditors nor your beneficiary's creditors can gain access to the Trust funds. The most a creditor can do is seek payment from the money that is received as an income.

☑   GOOD DEED

If you are concerned that your son will be tagged with a Capital Gains Tax once you die, it means that your property has appreciated more than 1.3 million dollars, and you are fortunate indeed. By setting up a Charitable Trust, you are making a donation to the charity of your choice. You are sharing your good fortune with others. You can consider this as "giving back" to the community, or just plain doing a good deed.

BECOME A PHILANTHROPIST

Instead of giving the property to an established charity, you can become a philanthropist and set up your own private IRS approved Charitable foundation. You can be the Trustee of the Charitable Remainder Annuity Trust and your child, the Successor Trustee. The Trust can be set up according to your specific charitable purposes. You can use the money to benefit a single cause or several worthy projects. This can be an exciting adventure for those with ample resources and a community spirit.

An Estate Plan For Your Person 8

The law makes a distinction between your property (what you own) and your person (your body). We have been discussing how to set up an Estate Plan for your property with the goal of maximum control over your Estate during your lifetime, and minimum cost and hassle to your heirs once you die. An Estate Plan for your body is just as important as an Estate Plan for your property. The goals are much the same. Maximum control over your body during your lifetime. Minimum cost and hassle to your family for your final disposition.

You may think it strange to speak of planning for maximum control of your body during your lifetime. After all, it's your body. Who else but you has any right to control what you do with your body? That may be true so long as you have capacity, but should you become seriously ill, you may be unable to express your wishes about the care you wish to receive. If you do not have an Estate Plan in place for your person, then your next of kin, or maybe the Commonwealth of Pennsylvania may make health decisions for you.

The same applies to the final disposition of your body. If you don't make Pre-need burial and/or funeral arrangements, then someone will need to make those decisions for you.

As this chapter will show, it is relatively simple and inexpensive to set up an Estate Plan for your person.

151

MAKING BURIAL ARRANGEMENTS

People with a large family often arrange for a family burial site. Over the years deceased family members come to occupy a space within that site, but others may have been buried elsewhere. Surviving family members may lose track of the number of spaces left. If this is the case with your family, then you need to take an inventory of the number of spaces available and who in the family expects to occupy those spaces.

It may be that the family burial site is not in Pennsylvania. In such case, it is important to consider the cost of transporting the body from Pennsylvania to the out of state cemetery. That cost can be substantial, in some cases doubling the cost of the burial. If there is no emotional attachment to the out of state burial site, you may want to consider assigning the burial site to a family member who lives closer to the site and making your own burial arrangements here in Pennsylvania.

If the burial site is within the state of Pennsylvania, it is important to keep in touch with the cemetery and let them know whenever there is a change in the identity of the intended occupant. Pennsylvania law requires an owner of a burial right to keep the cemetery informed of his current address. If, after 50 years, the cemetery is unable to locate the owner of the burial site after diligent effort, the burial site is considered to be abandoned. An abandoned site can once again be sold by the cemetery. If within 30 years from the date of abandonment, the owner, or his heirs, can prove that they are entitled to the burial site, the cemetery will provide another site, similar to the one that was abandoned, and at no charge to the owner or his heirs (9 P.S. 201).

You can achieve maximum control of the final disposition of your body by making your own burial and funeral arrangements. You can make preneed arrangements to be buried in the manner you wish and where your wish. Even if you don't particularly care where you are buried, it may be very important to your family.

That is often the case in second marriages. If you have children from a first marriage, they may want their parents to be "reunited in death." Your current spouse may not take kindly to having you buried with your former spouse. This might result in hard feelings, if not an out-and-out battle.

The same problem can arise with those in a gay relationship. The decedent's family may not have ever acknowledged the relationship. The family may decide to have the decedent buried in the family plot and exclude the gay partner from having any say in the burial arrangements.

You can head off disputes about your final resting place, by making your own burial arrangements. If you do not do so, then the person with authority to decide the matter for you is determined by the Commonwealth of Pennsylvania. Under Pennsylvania law, your surviving spouse has sole authority for your final disposition. If you are estranged from your spouse, or if you are single, then your next of kin, as determined by Pennsylvania's Laws of Intestate Succession has that authority (20 Pa.C.S.A. 305).

ARRANGING FOR CREMATION

Increasingly people are opting for cremation. The reasons for choosing cremation are varied, but for the majority, it is a matter of finances. The cost of cremation is approximately one-sixth that of an ordinary funeral and burial. A major saving is the cost of the casket. A casket is not necessary for the cremation. An alternate container of fiberboard or similar materials, can be used to transport the body. Embalming is not necessary either, unless there is to be a funeral with a viewing. Federal law prohibits a funeral director from saying that a casket or embalming is necessary for a direct (i.e., immediate) cremation (16 Code of Federal Regulations ("CFR") 453.3 (b)(1)(ii)).

For those who are considering cremation, there are a few things to consider.

THE PACEMAKER

Cremating a body with a pacemaker or any radiation producing device can cause damage to the cremation chamber and/or to the person performing the cremation. If you have such an electronic aid, it will need to be removed prior to the cremation. You might check with the cremation service to determine the cost of having the pacemaker removed. Incidentally, a pacemaker can be donated for use in animals with a medical need for the device. If you are interested in making such donation, you can ask you local veterinarian to refer you to an animal clinic that performs the procedure, and then tell your family that you wish to make the donation.

THE OVERWEIGHT

Cremation may not be an option for those who weigh more than 300 pounds. Many cremation services do not have the facilities to handle a large body. If you weigh more than 300 pounds, you need to check with your local cremation service to determine whether this will be a problem.

WHAT TO DO WITH THE ASHES

In addition to planning for the procedure, you need to give your family some guidance as to where to place the ashes. Some cemeteries allow an urn containing the cremated remains of a family member to be placed in an occupied family plot. Similarly, some cemeteries will allow the cremated remains to be placed in the space in a mausoleum that is currently occupied by a member of the decedent's family. If you intend to be cremated and all your family spaces are occupied you may want to call the cemetery and ask them to explain their policy as it relates to the burial of urns in occupied sites.

If burial in the family site is not an option, you will need to arrange for a separate burial space. Many cemeteries have a separate building called a *columbarium*, which is especially designed to store urns. You can purchase a storage place for the urn in the same manner as the purchase of a burial space in a cemetery.

If you wish to have your cremated remains scattered, then you need to let your next of kin know where and how this is to be done.

THE MILITARY BURIAL

If you are an honorably discharged veteran or the spouse of such veteran, you have the right to be buried in a Veterans National Cemetery. If your Veteran spouse was buried in a Veterans National Cemetery then you have the right to be buried in that same grave site unless soil conditions require a separate grave site.

You can get information about burial at a Veterans National Cemetery by calling the Veteran's Administration at (800) 827-1000, or visiting their Web site.

VA CEMETERY WEB SITE
http://www.cem.va.gov

The site has information on the following topics:
- ➢ National and Military Cemeteries
- ➢ Burial, Headstones and Markers
- ➢ State Cemetery Grants Program

You cannot reserve a grave site in advance, so your family will need to make arrangements and establish your eligibility to be buried in a Veterans National Cemetery. At that time, they will need to provide the following information:
- ➢ your rank, serial, social security and VA claim numbers
- ➢ the branch of service in which you served, the date and place of your entry into, and separation from, the service
- ➢ a copy of your official military discharge document bearing an official seal or a DD 214 form.

If you wish to be buried in a national cemetery, you need to make all of these items readily accessible to your family.

THE PRE-NEED PLAN

In addition to arranging a burial space, consider the purchase of a Pre-need Funeral Plan. It will be easier on your family emotionally and financially if you make your own funeral arrangements. If you do not have sufficient cash for the kind of funeral you desire, you might consider making payments on an installment plan.

Once you decide on a plan, the funeral director will present you with a contract. Even though the seller gives you a printed form, it does not mean that it cannot be changed. If you are not satisfied with the way a certain section of the contract reads, then attach an addendum to the contract that explains, in plain English, your understanding of that passage. If you are concerned about something that is not mentioned in the contract, then insist that the contract be amended to include that item.

In particular, check to see whether the contract answers the following questions.

Does the contract cover all costs?

The contract should contain an itemized list stating exactly what goods and services are included in the sales price. Ask the funeral director whether there will be any additional funeral or burial costs, such as printing an obituary, or purchasing death certificates. If you have not purchased a burial space, then that cost needs to be factored in. If you made provision for a burial space, then you need to let the funeral director know where you have arranged to be buried.

Is the price guaranteed?

Some Pre-need plans have a fixed price for the goods and services you choose. Such contracts guarantee that the goods and services purchased or items of the same style and quality will be provided upon your death, regardless of when you die. If you are buying a fixed price plan, you need to check out whether the person who is selling you the plan is the one who is going to provide the goods and services that you are purchasing. If not, have the seller of the contract attach his agreement with the company that is actually going to provide the goods and services to your contract. You may want to read such an agreement to be sure that the provider has agreed to honor your contract.

If the price for the goods and services that you have chosen under the Pre-need Funeral Plan is not fixed, then the company can charge additional monies upon your death. In these days of an ever increasing life expectancy, it is important that such a contract clearly state how the price will be determined when the contract is finally put into effect.

How are your contract funds protected?

Pennsylvania laws are designed to protect the purchaser of a Pre-need Funeral Plan. The seller is required to deposit 70% of the monies you pay into an interest bearing escrow or trust fund account. The trust account must be separate from the funeral director's business or personal account (49 Pa. Code of Regulations ("Pa.Code") 13.226).

You may want your contract to state that the company will, within 30 days, give you proof of deposit. You may also want the contract to require the seller to notify you, in writing, should he change the bank in which the trust fund is located.

Unless your contract provides differently, interest on the trust account goes to the seller (63 P.S. 480.5). You need to verify that the interest income will not be charged to you; else you will pay income tax on interest you never receive.

Is the funeral firm reputable?

All these precautions don't do much good if you are not dealing with a reputable company. It is important to take the time to check up on whoever is selling you the contract. In Pennsylvania, anyone who offers Pre-need Funeral contracts to the public must be licensed to do so. You can check to see if the seller is licensed by calling the **STATE BOARD OF FUNERAL DIRECTORS** at (717) 783-3397. You may also want to ask how long the company has been in business and whether any complaints have been filed against them.

Suppose you die in another state or country?

Your contract should spell out what provision will be made in the event that you move to another state or die in another state or country. Pennsylvania law requires that you have the right to cancel your contract and receive the monies held in the trust account, less the interest on that account which goes to the seller. Cancelling the contract can be expensive because only 70% of your contract price is required to be deposited into the Trust Account. Unless your contract states differently, you will forfeit 30% of what you paid.

Many funeral firms are part of a national funeral service corporation with funeral firms located throughout the United States. You may be able to have the contract provide that there will be no additional charge if the contract is performed by any one of the funeral firms owned by the parent company.

Can you cancel the contract?
It is important to read and understand that part of the contract that deals with your right to revoke the contract and get your money back. If you intend to pay for your Pre-need Funeral Contract on an installment basis, then you need to know how much of the monies you pay will be returned to you in the event that you default on payment.

FUNERAL PLANS FOR THOSE ON PUBLIC ASSISTANCE
People who are applying for, or receiving, Medicaid, Supplemental Security Income ("SSI") or other public assistance program have limits on the amount of assets that they may own. If someone purchases a Pre-need Funeral Plan, then the monies paid into the plan count as an asset because the purchaser of the plan can revoke the contract and get his money back. Understanding the problem, the Pennsylvania legislature included a provision in the law allowing the purchase of an Irrevocable Contract for those who need to apply for public assistance (55 Pa.Code 178.5).

If you are in the process of applying for a public assistance program, then before finalizing your funeral plan, it is prudent to check with your local Department of Public Welfare to be sure that your plan will not affect your ability to qualify for the program.

Even if you are in good health at this time, it is a good idea to have your contract provide that you can change your plan to conform to state and federal law, if at any time you need to apply for a public assistance program.

Can the plan be changed after your death?
It may happen that your heirs need to cancel the plan after your death because:
- ➢ your body is missing or cannot be recovered, or
- ➢ you were buried by another facility because no one knew that you had a Pre-need contract, or
- ➢ you died in another country and were buried there.

Your contract should address these potential problems, and spell out how much money will be refunded and who is to receive the refund.

You may also want to specify whether your heirs have the right to alter you funeral plans. In the absence of such a provision in the contract, funeral firms usually allow the family to arrange for a more expensive plan, provided they agree to pay the difference.

You may wonder why anyone would think of changing the decedent's funeral plan, but consider that in today's market, it is not uncommon for a Prearrangement Funeral Plan to cost several thousand dollars. A top end funeral complete with solid bronze casket can cost upwards of $30,000. Some heirs might be motivated to save money by changing the plan to one of a lesser value.

That was the case with Lester. His mother, Mona, was a difficult woman with a personality that can only be described as "sour." Her husband deserted her after four years of marriage leaving her to raise their Lester by herself. Once Lester was grown, Mona made it clear to him that she had done her job and now he was on his own. Lester could have used some help. He married and had three children. One of his children suffered with asthma and it was a constant struggle to keep up with the medical bills.

Mona believed in being good to herself. She did not intend to, nor did she, leave much money when she died. She knew that Lester would not be able to afford a "proper" burial for her, so she purchased a funeral plan and paid close to $18,000 for it. She was pleased when the funeral director told her that the monies would be kept safely in a trust account until the time they were needed.

Lester was not familiar with Pennsylvania law, so when Mona died he asked an attorney at the Legal Aid office to determine whether the Pre-need contract was revocable.

It was.

You know the ending to this story.

You may be thinking "Revocable. Irrevocable. All this contract stuff is giving me a headache. Why can't I just set aside some money and let my kids figure it out?"

The problem with that approach is that the cost of your final illness may leave you with little or no funds for your burial. To avoid the problem, you could purchase a life insurance policy to fund your funeral and burial, naming one or two trusted family members as the beneficiary of the policy. It is important that the person who is to receive the insurance funds clearly understands why he/she is named as beneficiary of the policy. It is equally important that the beneficiary agree to use the monies for the intended purpose.

It isn't so much that a family member is not trustworthy as it is that they may not understand what you intended — especially in those cases where other funds are available to pay for the funeral.

Too often insurance funds are left to a child who then refuses to contribute to the cost of the funeral saying in effect "Dad wanted me to have this money. That's why he left it to me."

To avoid a misunderstanding, put it in writing. It need not be a formal contract. It could be something as simple as a letter to the insurance beneficiary, with copies to your next of kin.

Dear Paul,

I purchased a $20,000 insurance policy today naming you as beneficiary of the policy. As we discussed this money is to be used to pay for the following:
- *my funeral; grave site and headstone*
- *perpetual care for my grave*
- *airfare for each of my grandchildren to attend the funeral*
- *dinner for the family after the wake*
- *lunch for the family after the funeral*

If there is any money left over, please accept it as my thanks for all the effort spent on my behalf.
  Love,
    Dad

P.S. I am sending a copy of this letter to your sister so that she will know that all arrangements have been made.

AN ESTATE PLAN FOR YOUR PERSON

Whether or not you arrange to pay for your burial or funeral, you need to let your next of kin know your feelings about the burial procedure. Let your family know whether you wish to be cremated or buried. If you wish to have a religious service, then let your family know the type of service and where it is to be held. Let the family know where you wish to be buried, or if you intend to be cremated, then where to place the ashes.

ANATOMICAL GIFTS

If you want to make an anatomical gift to take effect upon your death, you can make the gift as part of your Will; but it may be some time before your Will is located. The better route is to make the donation by a separate writing. You can complete a Donor Card when you apply for your Pennsylvania driver's license or Pennsylvania Identification Card. The Department of Transportation will not print the fact that you are a Donor on your driver's licence or identification card unless you give them permission to do so (20 Pa.C.S.A. 8613, 20 Pa.C.S.A. 8619).

GIFT FOR EDUCATION AND RESEARCH

Doctors will probably not consider your body suitable for transplantation if you are of advanced age, but you can still donate your body to a school of medicine or dentistry for education and research. The HUMAN GIFTS REGISTRY is a non-profit agency of the Commonwealth of Pennsylvania that coordinates donations among medical schools throughout the state. You can call them at (215) 922-4440 they will send you information about the program. Your Estate, or your family, will be responsible to pay for the transportation of your body to the school, so if you make such a gift, you need to give your family instructions about what to do in the event that you die far from home.

If you do not wish to make an anatomical gift, then let your family know how you feel. If you do not make provision for a gift, and do not tell anyone how you feel about donating any or all of your body, then the decision will be up to your family.

Pennsylvania statute gives an order of priority for those who can give permission to make an anatomical gift:
- 1st   spouse
- 2nd   adult son or daughter
- 3rd   either parent
- 4th   adult brother or sister
- 5th   the Guardian of the decedent at time of death
- 6th   anyone authorized to dispose of the body.

Pennsylvania law requires that every effort be made to contact those people with highest priority. If someone agrees to the gift and someone with higher priority objects, then no gift can be made. And Pennsylvania law prohibits the gift if the decedent, prior to death, refused to make a gift, or ever expressed an objection to someone with authority to make the gift (20 Pa.C.S.A. 8611).

AUTOPSIES

An autopsy is one of those things that most of us do not think about; reasoning that if it is needed, it will be carried out and, being dead, you will have no choice in the matter. But there are many times when an autopsy is optional. Sometimes a doctor is not sure of the cause of death, and asks the family to allow an autopsy. It is often in the family's best interest to consent to the autopsy. The examination might reveal a genetic disorder, that could be treated if it later appears in another family member. Death from a car "accident" could have been a heart attack at the wheel. Perhaps the patient who died suddenly in a hospital was misdiagnosed. The nursing home resident could have died from negligence and not old age.

Even if none of these are found, knowing the cause of death with certainty is better than not knowing.

The person giving authorization for an optional autopsy must agree to pay for the autopsy because the cost is not covered under most health insurance plans. An autopsy can cost anywhere from several hundred to several thousand dollars. Still another reason family members hesitate to allow the procedure is that they do not know how the decedent would have felt about the examination.

If you have strong feelings one way or another, then it is important to let your family know whether you would want an optional autopsy.

Of course, there are problems with just telling someone how you feel about your burial arrangements, autopsies, and anatomical gifts:

YOU TELL THE WRONG PERSON
You may tell someone who does not have authority to carry out your wishes. That was the case with James. When his wife died, he moved to a retirement community where he lived for several years until his death. James had two sons who lived in different states. Although he loved his sons, he had difficulty talking to either of them about serious matters. It was easier for him to talk with his friends in the retirement community. They often spoke about dying and how they felt about different burial arrangements. James would reminisce about his youth and growing up in a farming community in the plains state of Kansas. "I was happy and free. Out there you had room to breathe. It would be nice to be buried there — so peaceful and spacious."

When he died, his friends told his sons about their father's desire to be buried in Kansas. They met the suggestion with scepticism and pragmatism:

"Dad didn't say anything like that to me."

"It would cost us double, if we had to arrange for burial in another state. I'm sure he didn't have that kind of expense in mind."

THE PERSON DOES NOT CARRY OUT YOUR WISHES

Sometimes the person you tell about the disposition of your body may not understand what you said or perhaps they hear only what they want to hear. Whether they follow your burial instructions or authorize an autopsy or an anatomical gift may depend more about what costs are involved, and their own feelings, rather than what you may have wanted.

Even if you tell someone and trust that person to carry out your wishes, it could be that the person you confide in cannot carry out your instructions. For example, if you tell your spouse what arrangements to make, he/she may become incapacitated or die before you do; or perhaps you both die together in a natural disaster or in a plane crash.

WHO WANTS TO TALK ABOUT IT?

For many people the main problem with telling someone what to do when you die is talking about your death. It may be an uncomfortable, if not unpleasant, subject for you to bring up, and for your family to discuss. If this is the case, then consider putting the information in writing and give the instructions to the person who will have the job of carrying out your wishes.

APPOINTING A HEALTH CARE SURROGATE

Making provision for the disposition of your body is important, but it is more important to make sure that you are in control of the health care you receive should you become seriously ill. This is not a problem when you are well enough to make your own medical decisions; however it could happen that you are too ill to let people know what you want.

The solution to the problem is appoint someone to serve as your **Health Care Surrogate**. You can give your Surrogate instructions about medical treatment that you do, or do not, want to receive. You can give your Surrogate authority to see that your instructions are followed.

You can appoint a Health Care Surrogate by signing a document called an **Advance Directive For Health Care**. Pennsylvania statute (20 Pa.C.S.A. 5404) contains a statutory form that you can use to appoint a Health Care Surrogate to make your medical decisions in the event that you are too ill to do so yourself.

The statutory form contains a **Living Will** that tells your physicians whether you do (or do not) want life support systems to be used in the event that you are dying and there is no hope for your recovery.

You can have your attorney prepare an Advance Directive For Health Care to meet your special needs or you can prepare your own directive using the statutory form. You can look up the statute by going to the nearest courthouse law library. You can also download the form from the Pennsylvania statute Web site. See page viii for the Web site.

USING THE DIRECTIVE FOR ANATOMICAL GIFTS

If you want to make an anatomical gift, you can give your Health Care Surrogate authority to consent to the gift on your behalf. If you do not wish to make an anatomical gift, then you can indicate your refusal as part of your Advance Directive For Health Care.

USING THE DIRECTIVE FOR FINAL DISPOSITION

The statutory form of the Advance Directive for Health Care has a space for **OTHER INSTRUCTIONS**. You can use that space to authorize an autopsy, or you can direct your Surrogate to refuse the procedure, provided the autopsy is optional (35 P.S. 1111).

You can also use that space to give instructions about your final disposition and to give your Health Care Surrogate authority to carry out those instructions.

Some readers may not be convinced "Why bother with an Advance Directive? I probably will never need anyone to assist me. And even if I did, my family will tell the doctor what I want."

Those were George's thoughts exactly, even though his attorney advised him differently. George was a wealthy man. He was meticulous when it came to his business affairs, but not about his health care.

His attorney said "You made good provision for the care of your property in the event that you become disabled or die. You can sign an Advance Health Care Directive and appoint someone to be your Health Care Surrogate. Your Surrogate can make your medical decisions should it happen that you are too sick to make them yourself.

Your wife Loretta is a lovely lady, but she and your son from your first marriage are always at odds. You should give one of them the authority to serve as your Health Care Surrogate to make your medical decisions if you can't."

George refused. "No, if I make one my Surrogate, the other will be hurt."

The attorney persisted. "If you don't want to appoint a Health Care Surrogate, then at least let me prepare an Advance Directive For Health Care. It can give your doctor directions about the kind of medical treatment you want. For example, you can let them know whether you want intravenous feeding in the event that you are so ill that there is no hope of recovery."

"You mean sign a Living Will?"

"Yes, then at least you will be comfortable knowing that your wishes regarding whether you do or do not want intravenous feeding will be respected in such a situation."

George said he would think about it. But he didn't.

The attorney's advice turned out to be prophetic. George suffered a stroke while driving. His injuries from the accident combined with the severity of the stroke made for a bleak prognosis. The doctors said George would die unless they put him on a ventilator and inserted a feeding tube. Even with life support systems, it was not expected that he would ever come out of the coma.

Loretta told the doctors "Let's try everything to keep him alive."

George's son did not see it that way. "Why torture him with needles and tubes? Let him pass on peacefully."

George never signed an Advance Directive For Health Care, so no one knew how he felt about artificial life support systems. He never appointed a Health Care Surrogate, so the doctors didn't know who George wanted to speak on his behalf.

Fearing that no matter what they did, one family member might be angry enough to file a law suit, the doctors requested that the matter be brought before the court, to let the judge decide the matter.

The judge decided that someone needed to be appointed as George's Guardian to make his medical decisions.

Loretta petitioned the court to be appointed as George's Guardian. So did his son. The court battle that followed was both bitter and expensive.

Before Loretta and George married they signed a prenuptial agreement. The agreement provided for each to give up all rights to inherit property from the other. Loretta had little money of her own. The son accused Loretta of thinking of her own best interest and not that of his father. If George were to die, Loretta would be on her own.

George was a wealthy man, but he was not overly generous with his son. His son was married and raising his own family. Without any help from his father, he struggled to support his family. Loretta accused the son of being anxious to get his substantial inheritance.

The judge ruled that each of the parties had a conflict of interest and could be prejudiced by his/her own circumstances. He appointed a professional, independent, Guardian to make medical decisions for George. The Guardian conferred with the doctors and determined that it was futile to continue life support systems.

George died.

A Health Care Estate Plan 9

We have discussed an Estate Plan as it relates to the distribution or management of your Estate once you are deceased. But in this age of extended life expectancy, a more important topic is how to manage and preserve your Estate in the event of a debilitating illness. As life expectancy increases, so does the percentage of the population who suffer incapacity from debilitating strokes, Alzheimer's disease or Parkinson's disease. It is estimated that more than half of the population who are 85 or older, suffer some degree of dementia. Your best Estate Plan could be sabotaged by a lengthy or incapacitating illness. In this chapter we will explore ways to pay for the health care that you may require as you age.

In addition to paying for your health care, you need to consider who will care for your finances and everyday physical needs in the event that you are too ill to do so yourself. A *Health Care Estate Plan* is a plan designed to care for your person and property in the event of an incapacitating illness. In the last chapter we discussed how you can appoint a Health Care Surrogate to care for your person in the event of your incapacity.

But there is still the problem of who will care for your property. In this chapter we will discuss how you can appoint someone to care for your property and manage your finances in the event of your incapacity.

The optimum way to provide for the care of your property in the event of your incapacity is to set up a Trust appointing a Successor Trustee to care for your property according to the directions given in your Trust. You can be Trustee of the funds while you have capacity. Should you become incapacitated, then the person you name as Successor Trustee will take over. But if you do not have sufficient assets to justify the cost of employing an attorney to draft a Trust, then there are other strategies that you can use to solve the problem.

THE JOINT ACCOUNT
You can set up a joint checking account so that a trusted family member can write checks on the account. Of course there are all the inherent problems of a joint account that we discussed in Chapter 2. You can avoid many of those problems by limiting the amount of money that can be accessed by the family member. For example, you can arrange your finances so that all of your bills are paid from a single checking account and your family member can access that account, only.

THE AGENCY ACCOUNT
If you set up a joint account, your family member will own whatever is in the account should your die. If this is not as you wish, you can hold the account in your name only, and give your family member written authority to transact business with your account. The bank usually has a Power of Attorney form that you can sign when you open the account. The Power of Attorney form will specify that the family member may no longer access your account in the event of your death. But ultimately the family member must be trustworthy because the bank is under no duty to stop your family member from writing checks on your account until the bank learns of your death (7 P.S. 609).

GUARDIANSHIP: A GOOD THING TO AVOID

The joint or agency account solves the problem of how to pay your bills in the event you are temporarily ill. It does not solve the problem of how to manage your business affairs in the event of an extended illness. For example, suppose you have a stroke and can no longer be cared for at home. Should it be necessary for you to sell your home and move to an assisted living facility then no one will have the authority to sell the house for you. In such case, the Court will need to appoint a Guardian to manage your finances, and if you did not appoint a Health Care Surrogate, to make your health care decisions as well.

Setting up the guardianship is time consuming and expensive. Whoever believes you are unable to manage your person or property, can petition the Court to determine whether you need a Guardian. The Court will hold a Review Hearing to determine whether you need a Guardian. The person who filed the petition will need to present evidence that you are unable to care for your person or property.

You may have your own attorney to represent you at the hearing. If you cannot afford an attorney, and the Court determines that it is appropriate that you be represented, then the Court will appoint an attorney to represent you. (20 Pa.C.S.A. 5511, 20 Pa.C.S.A. 5518).

If the judge determines that you are incapacitated, he will appoint a Guardian of your person or property, or both. If a Guardian of your property is appointed he will take possession of your assets and file an inventory with the Court. The Court may order the Guardian of your property to obtain a bond for the protection of your assets (20 Pa.C.S.A. 5142, 20 Pa.C.S.A. 5516, 20 Pa.C.S.A. 5512.1).

The Court may require an annual accounting for monies spent. Your Guardian may need to employ an accountant to help prepare the inventory and annual accounting. Depending on the size of the Estate, the Guardian of the property may need to employ a financial advisor to manage your property.

If a Guardian of your person is appointed, he will see to your health care. He will need to prepare and file a report each year regarding your well-being (20 Pa.C.S.A. 5521). The Guardian will need to employ an attorney to establish the Guardianship and to see that reports are properly and timely filed.

The Guardian and his attorney are entitled to be paid for their services. Fees must be approved by the Court, but in general, the rate for the Guardian and his attorney are much the same as that for other fiduciaries such as Personal Representatives, and Trustees and their attorneys.

Court filing fees, the competency examination fee, the cost of a bond, accounting fees, the Guardian's fee, your attorney's fee and the Guardian's attorney fees, all are paid from your Estate (that's your money!)

Guardianship procedures are expensive to set up and maintain. Curious that so many people worry about how to avoid Probate, when the larger concern should be how to avoid guardianship. Consider that it is not all that hard to arrange your finances so that no Probate is necessary. The cost to transfer your property to your beneficiaries should be $0.

Even with a full Probate procedure, whatever it costs to Probate your Estate is a one-time expense. And Probate is a one-time procedure. Once monies are distributed to your beneficiaries, it is over. Not so if you become incapacitated. It can cost thousands of dollars to set up the Guardianship; and more money to care for you and your property each year. And this expense goes on, year after year, until you regain capacity, or die.

As with Probate it is not all that hard to avoid these unnecessary charges to your Estate. To avoid the need for a Guardian of your person, you can appoint a Health Care Surrogate to make your medical decisions should you be too ill to do so yourself.

To avoid the need for a Guardian of your property, you can set up a Trust and appoint a Successor Trustee to care for your property in the event of your incapacity. For those of limited means, the *Power of Attorney* is the next best Estate plan.

A POWER OF ATTORNEY FOR FINANCES

A Power of Attorney is a legal document by which someone (the **Principal**) gives another (his **Agent** or **Attorney-In-Fact**) authority to do certain acts on behalf of the Principal. Under Pennsylvania statute, unless the Power of Attorney states otherwise, it is considered to be *durable,* meaning that your Agent has the power to act on your behalf even if you later become disabled or incapacitated (20 Pa.C.S.A. 5601.1).

Pennsylvania statute (20 Pa.C.S.A. 5602) lists some 23 items that you can give your Agent authority to do on your behalf. The list includes the power to:

- engage in real property transactions;
- engage in banking and financial transactions;
- borrow money on your behalf;
- enter your safe deposit box;
- engage in insurance transactions;
- sue or defend a law suit on your behalf;
- prepare and file taxes on your behalf;
- apply for government benefits on your behalf;

Pennsylvania statute (20 Pa.C.S.A. 5603) goes on to explain exactly what your Agent can do if you give him such power. For example, if you give your Agent the power "to engage in real property transactions," then he can buy, sell, repair, restore, alter or do anything with your real property that you might do. This includes putting a mortgage on your home, selling it, or leasing it out and collecting rents on your behalf.

It is important that you do not give your Agent a specific power unless you know exactly what is included as part of that power under Pennsylvania law.

You can also give your Agent power to make gifts of your property in accordance with your Estate Plan, for example, you can direct him to give certain family members (spouse, children and their spouses) up to the amount allowed as an annual Gift Tax Exclusion (currently $11,000) (20 Pa.C.S.A. 5603).

Notice that there are many things that your Agent can do for you personally, such as suing or defending a law suit on your behalf or applying for government benefits. Even if you have a Trust, it is important to appoint an Agent under a Durable Power of Attorney to do these important, personal, things for you, in the event you can't. Your Trust can only authorize your Successor Trustee to manage property that is placed in your Trust. Your Successor Trustee has no authority over you, personally. But you can give him (or anyone else) that authority by making him your Agent under a Power of Attorney.

GENERAL VS. LIMITED POWER OF ATTORNEY

You can sign a Power of Attorney giving your Agent broad general powers. With these powers your Agent can do much the same with your property as you can. Instead of a General Power of Attorney, you can limit the things your Agent can do with your property to just those things that you authorize in your Power of Attorney.

One power that should be specifically granted in your Power of Attorney, is the power to apply for medical assistance benefits in the event of your incapacity. In the next chapter we will be discussing the many things you can do to qualify for Medicaid. You need to give someone authority to take the necessary steps for you to become eligible for government benefits, in the event you too ill to do so yourself.

A HEALTH CARE ESTATE PLAN   *179*

Even if you do not wish to give someone control over your finances at this time, you should give someone a Limited Power of Attorney with the power to apply for government benefits on your behalf.

Limited or General, the operative word in any Power of Attorney is POWER. Once your Agent has authority to act, he essentially steps into your shoes and can do whatever you gave him authority to do. Your primary consideration in choosing an Agent is trustworthiness. You need to choose someone who will follow your instructions and put the Power of Attorney to the use you intended. You need to choose someone, who, when using your Power of Attorney, will always put your interests ahead of his.

You may be less concerned with trustworthiness than the loss of independence. But the thing to keep in mind is that you still have the power to do all of the things you gave your Agent authority to do. The only difference is that now, you both have the power to conduct your business transactions.

Of course, shared authority is still less independent than sole authority; and you may hesitate to give someone a Power of Attorney until it is needed. But if you wait until it is needed, you may be too sick to sign the document. There are two solutions to this dilemma.

KEEP THE DOCUMENT IN YOUR POSSESSION

An Agent under a Power of Attorney cannot act for the Principal, unless the Agent has possession of the original Power of Attorney and presents it to whoever he asks to rely on that document. For example, if your Agent wants to use the Power of Attorney to sell one of your securities, he will need to produce the original document. He may also be asked to sign an Affidavit saying that the Power of Attorney is still in effect and that you did not revoke it (20 Pa.C.S.A. 5606). If you keep the original document in your possession and do not give anyone a copy, your Agent will not be able to transact business on your behalf. The only problem with this arrangement is that you need to make the document accessible to your Agent in the event of your incapacity. If your Agent is a trusted family member, then you can give your Agent the location of the document with instructions to take possession of the Durable Power of Attorney in the event of your incapacity.

THE SPRINGING POWER OF ATTORNEY

A better solution may be to have your attorney draft a "springing" Durable Power of Attorney that is not operational until your family doctor and/or independent physician says that you are incapacitated and unable to manage your financial affairs. Your Agent can hold the original document, but cannot use it until it "springs to life" when a doctor determines that you are too ill to care for your property. You can create a Springing Durable Power of Attorney by adding the following provision to the document:

> This Durable Power of Attorney becomes operational only when my regularly attending physician and _____ (name of family member) sign an Affidavit stating that I am disabled or incapacitated.

USING THE POWER OF ATTORNEY FOR HEALTH CARE

Your attorney can design a Durable Power of Attorney, to meet your special needs. He can even include powers relating to your health care, such as authorizing medical and surgical procedures. But as a practical matter, it may be better to have a separate Power of Attorney for Health Care, or appoint a Surrogate under an Advance Directive for Health Care to make your medical decisions only if you are unable to do so yourself. There are two reasons to have a separate Health Care Directive:

APPOINT DIFFERENT PEOPLE TO SERVE
You may want one person to serve as your Health Care Surrogate and another to serve as your Agent. One family member may be an excellent choice to make your health care decisions, yet that person may not be the best person to make financial decisions on your behalf.

PRIVACY
Even if you want the same person to serve as your Health Care Surrogate and Agent, there is still the matter of privacy. Your Health Care Surrogate will give a copy of your Advance Directive for Health Care to your physician to be placed in your medical file. Your doctors have no need to know of your business dealings; and vice versa. To conduct business on your behalf your Agent will need to give a copy of the Power of Attorney to your business associates (banks, stockbrokers, etc.). Your business associates have no need to know of your medical decisions.

For privacy, and perhaps security reasons, consider having a separate Health Care Advance Directive (or Power of Attorney for Health Care) and a separate Power of Attorney for finances, rather than try to get it all into a single multi-purpose document.

CARING FOR YOU WHEN YOU CAN'T

It is relatively simple and inexpensive to head off guardianship. All you need do is appoint an Agent under a Durable Power of Attorney to manage your finances, and a Health Care Surrogate to make your medical care decisions under an Advance Directive for Health Care. These documents authorize people of your choice to care for you and your property in the event of your incapacity. But, despite your best plans, something unusual could happen requiring a Court to decide that you need a Guardian. For example, suppose you disappear and cannot be found after a diligent search. It might be necessary to have a Court appoint a Trustee to care for your property with the same rights and duties as a Guardian (20 Pa.C.S.A. 5702). Or you could develop an addiction or a mental illness causing self-destructive behavior. Your friends or family might decide that you are in need of protection and ask a Court to appoint a Guardian to care for you.

Although it may not be possible to avoid all guardianship procedures, you can have a measure of control over your fate. Pennsylvania statute gives you the right to name the person of your choice to serve as your Guardian (20 Pa.C.S.A. 5604). You can do this by having your attorney prepare a Durable Power of Attorney naming someone to serve as your Guardian should the need arise. Your attorney could include such a provision in a Power of Attorney prepared to handle your financial matters; however, as discussed on the prior page, it may be a better idea to prepare a separate Power of Attorney to give to the Guardian of your choice. Should a guardianship procedure be necessary, he can present the original document to the Court. All things being equal, the Judge will honor your wishes and appoint the person of your choice to serve as your Guardian.

PROVIDING FOR LONG TERM CARE

The good news is: You are going to live longer.
The bad news is: It's going to cost you.

Scientists are doing a great job of prolonging life, but unless they find Ponce De Leon's fountain, the general population will age. Along with age comes infirmities. Eyes fail. Hearing diminishes. Mobility declines. Digestive systems either speed up or slow down, all to the discomfort of the unhappy occupant of the body. It's all part of the "golden" years.

The pharmacology industry is well motivated to produce drugs that manage the ills associated with aging. Their research has led to a wealth of pharmaceutic products that do not cure, but do allow people to live relatively comfortably into advanced age. The only problem is the cost of these drugs. Medicare covers the treatment of life-threatening brushes with heart disease, stroke, cancer and diabetes; but, as of this writing, Medicare does not pay for maintenance medication that is often necessary once the condition is stabilized.

Medicare is also limited in long term care coverage. It does not pay for extended nursing care. Medicare pays for the first 20 days of skilled nursing care. Medicare pays the excess over $101.50** for days 21 through 100. That means it is your responsibility to pay $8,120 for the next 80 days. After 100 days, you are on your own. A nursing home stay of one or two years can wipe out the life savings of most working people. Once savings are gone, the government provides care in the form of Medicaid coverage.

**This is the value as we went to print. The federal government adjusts the amount each year.

If you have no assets to speak of, and an income beneath the poverty level, then the cost of long-term nursing care is the least of your worries. Medicaid is available to take care of your medical and nursing care needs. And no need to worry if you are wealthy. You have enough money to pay for any care that you might need. The rest of us need to think about ways to provide for long-term health care.

For those concerned about the loss of life savings because of illness, there is supplemental and/or long-term health care insurance. There are many different insurance plans available. You can call the National Association of Insurance Commissioners at (816) 842-3600 and they will forward to you, free of charge, the publication:
 A SHOPPER'S GUIDE TO LONG TERM CARE INSURANCE

If you have a specific question about long-term care insurance, you can call the PENNSYLVANIA DEPARTMENT OF AGING at (717) 783-8975.

LONG-TERM CARE INSURANCE FOR FEDERAL EMPLOYEES

The Long Term Care Security Act (Public Law 106-265) was passed by Congress to take effect as of October, 2002. The law is designed to make long term care insurance available to federal and postal employees, members of the uniformed services, civilian and military retirees, and their qualified relatives. You can call the Office of Personnel Management at (800) 582-3337 for information about the program or visit their Web site.

OFFICE OF PERSONNEL MANAGEMENT
http://www.opm.gov/insure/ltc

The National Association Of Retired Federal Employees ("NARFE") has been actively involved in developing this legislation. You can get information about the program at the NARFE office in Alexandria, Virginia at (703) 838-7780 or you can get information from their Web site.

    NARFE WEB SITE
    http://www.narfe.org

THE PROBLEM OF COST AND ELIGIBILITY

Long term care insurance sounds like the perfect solution, until you start examining the cost. The cost isn't too bad if you are comparatively young, say in your 50s. But can you imagine paying that premium each month until you are in your 80s and never needing nursing care?

Many decide to wait till they are old and going downhill. But that just brings other problems. The older you are, the greater the cost of insurance. And there is the risk that you will be refused coverage because of a "pre-existing" condition, i.e., the insurance company may consider you to be too great a risk for them to insure.

Different insurance companies have come up with insurance plans that may provide a solution for the person who is relatively young and in good health. Some companies offer long-term care insurance that is paid-up within a fixed period of time. Once payments are made for a certain number of years, the person is insured for long-term care without further payment. Other companies combine long-term care insurance with a life insurance policy. They offer long-term care insurance that converts to a life insurance policy, if it happens that the insured person dies before needing long-term care. When shopping for a long-term care policy, consider including different insurance alternatives in your investigation.

WHEN INSURANCE IS NOT AN OPTION

For some people long term care insurance is not an option. An elderly person living on a low fixed income may not have enough money to pay the monthly premium for a long term care insurance policy. And long term care insurance is not an option for the person who has been diagnosed with a chronic, debilitating disease.

People in such a position worry that they may need to deplete their life savings, just to pay for a year or two of nursing care.

Both of these problems can be solved by using current law to become qualified for Medicaid. Medicaid is a public assistance program that is funded jointly by the federal and state government. There are state and federal laws governing who may become eligible for the program.

A ***Medicaid Qualifying Plan*** is a plan that takes both state and federal laws into consideration. Operating within the boundaries of these laws, those who are concerned about becoming impoverished in order to pay for long-term care, seek to preserve and protect their Estate by implementing a Medicaid Qualifying Plan.

There has been controversy about plans designed to qualify a person for Medicaid. Some think that to intentionally arrange finances to qualify for Medicaid is immoral — a legal method of working the system.

Those people may argue: "Why are such things allowed? After all, wasn't Medicaid designed to help <u>poor</u> people? Why should people be allowed to make themselves poor to get on the public dole??

Those who feel they need to qualify for Medicaid have a different point of view. They may argue:

"I worked all my life and hoped to leave a few pennies for the kids. Why did I work so hard? To give it all to a nursing home? I paid my taxes just like everyone else. The government pays hundreds of thousands of dollars for people on Medicare to have open heart surgery, and they pay for lengthy and expensive cancer treatments. Why should those who have Alzheimer's or Parkinson's or those who suffer a debilitating stroke, not be entitled to receive equal benefits?"

Although we can understand and appreciate both points of view, our job, as we see it, is to just explain the law as it is at the time of publication. We feel that it is important to do so because many people take a position (pro or con) based on what they perceive the law to be, and not based upon the law as it actually is.

Once the reader understands what it takes to qualify for Medicaid in the Commonwealth of Pennsylvania, he can decide for himself whether the law is basically fair to the people who need to qualify, or whether it is flawed (either too restrictive or too liberal) and needs to be changed.

Hopefully, those with a strong opinion will share those views with their legislators.

A Medicaid Qualifying Plan   10

A better name for this chapter might be "A Health Care Contingency Plan." A lengthy stay in a nursing home is something most of us do not want to even think about, much less prepare for. Why prepare for something that may never happen? Yet as we age, there is that nagging "What if?" "What if I need long term nursing care? How will I pay for it?"

An effective way to put this anxiety at rest is to have a contingency plan. To form a contingency plan, you need to know your options. In this case, your options are directly related to your ability to pay for that care. But it is hard to predict future fortunes. People win the lottery. Those with a large portfolio may have their fortunes disappear in a market melt-down. There is no need for concern if it turns out that you can afford to pay for your own nursing care; and there is no concern should you become impoverished because there are government programs that provide for your health care. The worst case scenario is that you will be able to afford long-term care, but at the cost of your life savings.

In this chapter we will discuss options available to you under that worst case scenario. We will explain current state and federal law as it relates to qualifying for medical assistance programs.

Once you know the law, you will be able to form a contingency health care plan that is right for you.

WHO IS ENTITLED TO MEDICAID?

Medicaid is a program that provides medical and long term nursing care for people with low income and limited resources. The program is funded and regulated by both federal and state government. The governing agency for the federal government is the Centers for Medicare and Medical Assistance Programs Services. The Department of Public Welfare is the state governing agency for the Medicaid program. Applications are taken and the program administered at the local level by the COUNTY ASSISTANCE OFFICE.

Medicaid is an entitlement program, meaning that whoever qualifies for the program is entitled to receive benefits under that program, and conversely those who do not qualify are not entitled to Medicaid benefits. In Pennsylvania, Medicaid is included as part of the state's MEDICAL ASSISTANCE PROGRAMS.

There are many benefits offered under Pennsylvania's Medical Assistance Programs, from health care for mothers and children; to community based services for those who need some assistance with their health care; to full nursing care for those who need assistance with dressing, bathing, feeding, walking and toileting. We will limit our discussion of Pennsylvania's Medical Assistance Programs to those who need institutional nursing care. You can get information about other programs by calling the Office of Medical Assistance Programs at (717) 787-1870. You can also get information about Medical Assistance Programs from their Web site.

OFFICE OF MEDICAL ASSISTANCE PROGRAMS
http://www.dpw.state.pa.us/omap

Persons who are receiving Supplemental Security Income ("SSI") may be eligible to receive Medical Assistance benefits because the requirements for these programs are much the same. If a person is not receiving SSI, he may be eligible for Medical Assistance Programs if he is 65 or older, or blind, or permanently and totally disabled (55 Pa.Code 141.81).

When a person applies for Medical Assistance Programs (the "Applicant"**), the County Assistance Office ("CAO") will investigate his medical condition, income, and assets. If the Applicant is too ill to apply for himself, his spouse, relative, guardian or friend may apply for him (42 CFR 435.908, 62 P.S. 446, 55 Pa.Code 125.84).

MEDICAL ELIGIBILITY

Generally, an Applicant who is currently receiving institutional care is medically eligible for Medical Assistance Programs. However, if there is any question regarding his condition, a Review Team will review the Applicant's medical report to determine whether he requires institutional care (42 CFR 435.541).

In Pennsylvania the Review Team is composed of a County Medical Consultant and a qualified member of the Income Maintenance staff (55 Pa.Code 141.81).

** For simplicity, we will use the male gender for the Applicant and the female gender for his spouse.

INCOME ELIGIBILITY

In Pennsylvania, there is a limit on the amount of income earned by the Applicant each month, but that limit takes the cost of nursing care into consideration so it is quite high (currently about $8,000) (55 Pa.Code 181.12). An Applicant with an income greater than $8,000 could afford to pay for his own nursing care, so there would be no need for him to apply for Medical Assistance.

THE PERSONAL NEEDS ALLOWANCE
Once the Applicant is approved and becomes a recipient of Medicaid benefits (i.e. a **Medicaid Recipient**), his income will be used to supplement the cost of his nursing care. The Recipient is allowed to keep a certain amount of his income each month (currently $30) for his personal needs, such as clothing or hair cuts (55 Pa.Code 181.452).

RESOURCE ELIGIBILITY

In addition to income limits, there are limits to the Applicant's **Resources**. A Resource is anything owned by the Applicant, or his spouse, that can be converted to cash and used for their support. This includes bank accounts, certificates of deposit, property in a Revocable Living Trust, stocks, bonds, etc. (55 Pa.Code 178.4).

The Applicant may have no more than $2,400 in Resources. An Applicant who is over the Resource limit when he applies for Medical Assistance Programs needs to "spend down" to $2,400.

If the Applicant is married, there are limits to his spouse's Resources as well. If his spouse lives in a home in the community (i.e., not in a nursing home), she is referred to as the **Community Spouse**.

Prior to 1988, the Community Spouse was required to use whatever assets she had to pay for the nursing care of her spouse. The Applicant could not quality for Medicaid until they both were virtually impoverished. In addition to being unfair to the Community Spouse, this was not good government policy because it often resulted in the impoverished spouse turning to local government social service programs for support.

The Medicaid provisions of the Medicare Catastrophic Coverage Act of 1988 remedied the situation by considering the assets of the couple as being part of a common pot and allowing the Community Spouse to keep up to $90,660 of their combined Resources.

The federal government also considers that the Community Spouse needs money each month for her maintenance. If her income is not sufficient to support her, the income of the Medicaid Recipient will be used to supplement the income of the Community Spouse up to a maximum of $2,267 per month. The federal government adjusts the Resource Allowance and the Monthly Maintenance Allowance annually for cost of living increases (42 U.S.C. 1382b).

Notice that $90,660 and $2,267 are the maximum values set by the federal government for the year 2003. States have the right to administer the Medicaid program according to their state law, provided their state law is within federal guidelines and does not exceed the maximum values set by the federal government. This being the case, the actual amount allowed to the Community Spouse can vary significantly state to state.

THE SPOUSE'S RESOURCE ALLOWANCE

Resources owned by the Applicant or his spouse, are considered to be available to the Applicant for purposes of Medical Assistance Programs eligibility. Under federal law, the Community Spouse is entitled to keep a share of the couple Resources up to the current maximum of $90,660. That share is called the **Community Spouse Resource Allowance** (42 U.S.C. 1396r-5(c)(2), 1396r-5f).

In Pennsylvania, the Community Spouse is allowed to keep half of their common pot of assets with a minimum value of $18,132 up to the federal maximum value of $90,660. For example, suppose the couple own $20,000 between them. The Community Spouse is allowed to keep $18,132 as her Resource Allowance. The Applicant is allowed to keep the remainder as part of his $2,400 Resource Allowance. All other things being equal, the Applicant should qualify for Medical Assistance Programs.

But suppose the couple have $150,000 worth of assets between them. In that case, the Community Spouse can keep her half ($75,000) as a Resource Allowance. The Applicant can keep his $2,400, but that leaves them with $72,600 above the federal Resource limit of $90,660.

The first question to ask in such a situation is whether the Community Spouse has enough money to support herself each month. As explained, the state and federal government set limits for the income of the Community Spouse.

THE SPOUSE'S INCOME

The current value set by the state of Pennsylvania as the Community Spouse's **Minimum Need Allowance** is $1,505. Included in this value is a shelter allowance for rent, mortgage, property taxes, homeowner's insurance, utilities etc. If the shelter expenses of the Community Spouse are higher than allowed under Pennsylvania law, then the spouse may keep up to $762 as an *excess shelter allowance.* In other words, the most the Community Spouse is allowed as a Maintenance Need Allowance is the federal value of $2,267. If for some reason (high medical bills, the need for special care, etc.), the spouse needs more than $2,267 a month, she can appeal to have that value increased. See the next chapter for a discussion of the appeal process.

Once the application for Medical Assistance is filed with CAO, they will determine the amount allotted to the Community Spouse each month as the Minimum Need Allowance. If the Community Spouse's monthly income from her job or from social security, pension, etc., is greater than that value, then none of the Applicant's income is available to the Community Spouse. All of his income will be put towards the cost of his care.

If the Community Spouse's monthly income is less than the amount determined by CAO as her Minimum Need Allowance, then she may be allowed to keep as much of the couple's excess Resources as necessary to get her to that minimum value. If the couple do not have excess Resources or if their Resources are not enough to generate the required income, CAO will allow the Community Spouse to keep as much of the Applicant's income each month as is necessary to get her to that minimum value.

GENERATING THE EXTRA INCOME

The CAO will allow the Community Spouse who has too little income and too much in Resources, to keep as much of those excess Resources as is necessary to get to her Minimum Need Allowance. CAO computes the amount she can keep based on the going rate for an investment in a commercial annuity. They use tables based on the income currently being paid by commercial annuities to determine how much income can be generated by keeping additional Resources.

For example, suppose the Community Spouse in the previous example who was over the Resource Limit $72,600, did not have enough income to get her to the Minimum Need Allowance as determined by CAO. If CAO determines that she needs $20,000 to generate enough income to get her to that Minimum Need Allowance, she can keep that additional money and it will not count as a Resource. She can use the money to buy an annuity, or she can invest it in a stock, bond, Certificate of Deposit, etc.

The $20,000 needed to generate additional income does not count as a Resource, however, our couple is still over the Resource limit by $52,600. The next question to ask is whether the couple own other assets that do not count as a Resource.

WHAT COUNTS AS A RESOURCE?

Resources are assets owned by the Applicant, either by himself or together with another, that are countable for purposes of qualifying for Medical Assistance Programs. The federal and state government consider certain items to as "Excluded Assets" or "Non-Countable Resources." We will refer to them as *Exempt Resources* (42 U.S.C. 1382b). The following items are Exempt Resources and are not counted as a Resource for purposes of determining eligibility for Pennsylvania's Medical Assistance Programs.

PERSONAL PROPERTY
Basic items being used for everyday living by the Applicant or his spouse are exempt items. They include:
- personal effects of limited value, including clothing, jewelry and items of personal care
- household furnishings and appliances
- recreational equipment, musical instruments
- equipment needed for rehabilitation or for self-care (55 Pa.Code 178.66).

THE HOME
- The primary residence (home, condominium, cooperative apartment, or mobile home) that is occupied by the Applicant or his family (spouse, minor or dependent child, dependent relative) is an Exempt Resource.

The Applicant's home is an Exempt Resource so long as it is his primary residence or that of a family member. If the Applicant is in a nursing home, and no family member lives in the home, it remains an Exempt Resource, provided the Applicant has indicated that he intends to return home (42 U.S.C. 1382b, 55 Pa.Code 178.62).

AUTOMOBILE
One car, regardless of its value, is an Exempt Resource. The *equity value* (market value less monies owed) of a second car counts as a Resource (55 Pa.Code 178.67).

LIFE INSURANCE
⇨ An insurance policy owned by the Applicant is an Excluded Resource, provided its face value (the amount paid at death) is $1,500 or less. If the Applicant owns more than one policy on the same person, then they are Excluded Resources, provided the sum of their face values is not greater than $1,500. If the total face value death benefit of life insurance on any one person, is more than $1,500, then anything over the first $1,000 of the Cash Surrender Value of the policy (or policies) counts as a Resource.

⇨ A term insurance policy does not have a cash surrender value, so it is an Exempt Resource, regardless of its face value (55 Pa.Code 178.69, 178.70).

BURIAL ARRANGEMENTS
⇨ A burial space, crypt, mausoleum, urn and grave marker for the Applicant or family member (spouse, child, parent, sibling, etc.) is an Exempt Resource.

⇨ An Irrevocable Pre-Need Funeral Agreement, as described on page 160, is an Exempt Resource.

⇨ A burial fund of up to $1,500 is excluded, provided the fund is in a separate account and is clearly identified as a burial fund for the Applicant. The Community Spouse's burial fund (up to $1,500) is also an Exempt Resource (55 Pa.Code 178.2, 55 Pa.Code 178.5, 55 Pa.Code 178.71, 55 Pa.Code 178.73).

INCOME PRODUCING PROPERTY

Property which is essential to the self-support of the Applicant or his spouse or his dependents is an Exempt Resource. This includes business equipment (computers, copiers, etc.), special tools, farm equipment and work vehicles (tractors, trucks, etc.), animals and livestock (55 Pa.Code 178.64, 55 Pa.Code 178.65).

PENSION PLAN

The cash value of the Applicant's pension plan counts as a resource, however, his spouse's pension plan (including IRA's) is an Exempt Resource (55 Pa.Code 178.91).

ASSETS THAT ARE NOT SALEABLE

Property owned by the Applicant or his spouse must be able to be converted to cash in order to be counted as a Resource. Shares held in a close corporation, certain irrevocable annuities, and other non-saleable items can be considered as Exempt Resources. Real property owned jointly by the Applicant and another (not his spouse) does not count as a Resource provided the property cannot be sold without permission from the joint owner, and the joint owner refuses to sell (55 Pa.Code 178.4).

JOINTLY OWNED BANK ACCOUNT

The CAO considers the full value of a jointly owned bank account to be available to the Applicant, or his spouse; unless it can be proven that the other owner contributed money to the account. For example, if the Applicant owns a joint account with his son, the entire balance counts as a Resource unless the son can prove that he contributed his own money to that account. The son's net contribution (how much he contributed less how much he withdrew) does not count as a Resource (55 Pa.Code 178.51).

OTHER EXEMPT ASSETS

We have listed many of the more common items that the CAO considers to be Exempt Resources. But this is not a complete list. There are other items that the CAO will not count as part of the Applicant's Resources. An experienced Elder Law Attorney will be able to examine all of the property owned by Applicant and his Community Spouse and tell him what assets the CAO considers to be an Exempt Resource.

Now that we know what does (and does not) count as a Resource, the next question is what options are available to a couple who is over the Resource limit. Those with no knowledge of the law, might think the only option available to the couple is to pay for his nursing care until the money runs out. Those who carefully read the previous pages, might suggest that the couple check to see whether they can use the money to purchase items that do not count as a Resource.

THE SPEND-DOWN OPTION

Both state and federal law allow the Applicant and his spouse to use their excess Resources to purchase Exempt Resources, without losing the right to receive Medical Assistance benefits, provided they pay a fair market value for the item. This being the case, the couple can make funeral or burial arrangements, if they have not already done so. They can purchase household items such as furniture, a television set, a new refrigerator or stove, etc.

◇ REPAIR EXEMPT ITEMS

Paying money to repair exempt items is a good spend-down strategy. Perhaps the exempt family car needs new brakes, or tires. The Community Spouse may decide to replace the car with a new model. If the house is in need of repair or improvement, then this is the time to fix it up. A new heating, plumbing or electrical system can use up funds quickly.

If the couple do not own their own home, the Community Spouse might consider using the excess cash as a down-payment on a home.

◇ SPEND-DOWN BY PAYING DEBTS

Spending down by buying or repairing Exempt Resources may not be an option for the couple with assets over the Resource limit. Maybe the couple previously made all funeral arrangements. Perhaps they really don't need (or want) new furniture or appliances. In such case, the solution may be to pay off all of their outstanding debts. If the couple have a credit card balance, they can reduce the balance to $0. If their car is an Exempt Resource, they can pay off any money they may owe on the car.

Paying off loans is a valid spend-down strategy because it is just a return of monies given to the Applicant by the lender for the purchase of an Exempt Resource (car, house, clothing, household items).

The Applicant will need to prove to the CAO, that the monies he spent were used to pay off a valid debt. If a car loan was paid, the CAO will want to see the original promissory note (marked "PAID"), as well as other loan items, such as a chattel mortgage. If the money was used to pay down a mortgage on his home, the CAO will want to see the original loan documents as well as documents showing the new balance, or a satisfaction of mortgage, if it was paid in full.

CAUTION   TIMING IS IMPORTANT WHEN SPENDING DOWN

The couple's Resources are counted as of the day that the Applicant entered the nursing home. That date is called the **Snap Shot Date** because the CAO takes a "picture" of their assets on that date (42 U.S.C. 1396r-5(f)(2)). If a couple have $150,000 and a mortgage of $75,000 on the Snap Shot Date, the Applicant can apply for Medical Assistance. He will not qualify because they are over the Resource limit, however they can pay down the mortgage and qualify the next month.

It is best not to spend down before applying for Medical Assistance because the amount the Community Spouse is allowed to keep depends on their Resources as of the Snap Shot Date. The Community Spouse will be allowed to keep half of the $150,000 or $75,000. The Applicant is allowed to keep $2,400. They can use the remaining $72,600 to reduce the size of their mortgage.

Suppose instead that they pay the mortgage before the Snap Shot date. In that case, they will have $75,000 left. This leaves them in a worse position because the CAO will allow the Community Spouse to keep half of the $75,000 (only $37,500). The Applicant will be allowed to keep his $2,400, but he will be over the Resource limit by $35,100 and will need to spend down in some other manner.

The same concerns arise when buying Exempt Resources or making repairs. If a married Applicant spends down before the Snap Shot Date, the Community Spouse may be left with less assets than if they had spent down after that date.

Before using any spend down strategy, it is best to consult with an Elder Law attorney to determine the best course of action.

OPTIONS FOR THE SINGLE APPLICANT

Spend-down may not be the best strategy for the single Applicant with significant assets such as the father who has $100,000. Sure he can make his funeral arrangements; but that will only use up a small portion of his assets. He could buy an expensive car, but what good would that be if he needs to enter a nursing home?

If the Applicant has a medical condition that does not require immediate nursing care, he may decide to simply transfer all of his money to his child. The CAO will consider this to be an *uncompensated transfer* i.e. the Applicant gets nothing in return for the transfer (love and affection don't count).

Should the Applicant go this route, the CAO will impose a penalty period based on the amount of money transferred.

COMPUTING THE PENALTY PERIOD

The penalty period is computed by dividing the amount transferred by the average monthly cost of nursing home care in the Commonwealth of Pennsylvania (55 Pa.Code 178.104). The value for the average monthly cost of nursing care currently being used by the CAO is $5,313.18. If the Applicant, in the example just given, decided to transfer all of his $100,000 to his child he would be disqualified for 18 months:
$100,000/$5,313.18 = 18.82 or 18 months

The CAO currently rounds down to the nearest month, however, state legislators have proposed that the fraction be included. If they pass that rule, then the penalty period will be 18 months, 24.6 days:
30 X .82 days = 24.6 days

THE RULE OF HALVES

The strategy of transferring all his assets and waiting eighteen months may not be an option if our single Applicant needs immediate nursing care. In such case, the adage "half a loaf is better than none" applies; only in legal circles we refer to it as the **Rule of Halves**. The concept is simple. The Applicant gives away a certain amount of money to trigger a penalty period for a certain amount of time and yet keeping enough money for his care during the penalty period. For example, suppose our single Applicant who has $100,000 finds that he needs $5,300 month (in addition to his ordinary income) to pay for his nursing care and living expenses. If the average cost of nursing care is $5,313.18 and the Applicant gives half of his assets to his child it will trigger a nine month penalty period: $50,000/$5,313.18 = 9.41 or 9 months.

During that penalty period the Applicant will use the remaining $50,000 to pay for his nursing care and living expenses. At the end of 9 months he should have no assets left and can apply for Medicaid. He will report the $50,000 transfer to the CAO, and they will note that the penalty period has passed. All other things equal, the Applicant should qualify for Medicaid at that time.

Of course, in the real world, he may need more or less than $5,300 to supplement his income each month. The amount he gives away needs to be adjusted accordingly.

Although the Rule of Halves is easy to understand, implementing it needs careful consideration. It is important to consult with an Elder Law attorney who can calculate the proper balance between gift and monies that need to be reserved for the Applicant's care during the penalty period.

JUST GIVE IT ALL AWAY

The strategy we have been discussing can be used if the Applicant needs nursing care in the near future. But it may happen that a person is diagnosed in the early stages of a progressive disease that is expected to ultimately result in a lengthy stay in a nursing facility. A person in such a situation may decide to give his property away, with the hope that he will not need long term nursing care for at least three years.

The three years is the *look-back period* that the CAO uses to investigate the finances of a person who applies for Medical Assistance Programs. The look-back period increases to five years from the date of application if there was a transfer into a Trust (42 U.S.C. 1396p(c); 55 Pa.Code 178.104). If the CAO determines that the Applicant, or his spouse, made uncompensated transfers during the look-back period, the CAO will impose a penalty period based on the value of the transfer.

CAUTION THERE IS NO LIMIT ON THE PENALTY PERIOD

Although the CAO will only look back 3 years for transfers, there is no limit on the penalty period imposed for that transfer. For example, suppose the Applicant gives his child $300,000. If he applies for Medical Assistance Programs within three years from the date of transfer, he can be denied Medical Assistance Programs benefits for well over four years:

$300,000/$5,313.18 = 56 months or 4.67 years

Of course the way to avoid the problem is to transfer the funds and not apply any sooner than three full years from the date of the transfer. But if the transfer was made into an irrevocable Trust, the Applicant is stuck with the full 56 months because, as explained, the state has the right to look back 5 years and impose the full penalty for transfers into a Trust.

And this is not a game of "Catch me if you can." Under both state and federal law, the Applicant and his spouse (or whoever applies for him) are required to make a full disclosure of transfers made during these periods. Anyone who knowingly and wilfully makes a false statement in an application for Medical Assistance Programs can be prosecuted for fraud. If convicted he can be found guilty of a 3rd degree felony; fined up to $15,000 and imprisoned up to 7 years AND the Medicaid Recipient can be required to repay the state for benefits that were received improperly (55 Pa.Code 1101.92, 55 Pa.Code 1101.93).

The reader may be thinking "Yes, but if I don't make a transfer into a Trust, all the law requires is that I report transfers made within the previous 3 years. If I come down with an illness that I know will cause me to deteriorate over a period of time, all I need do is give all my money to my child; be sure to wait three years and I will qualify for Medical Assistance Programs. My child will keep my money safe. Should I need that money, my child will return as much as I need to me. Money that I don't use will be protected for my child."

The Medical Assistance Programs Qualifying Plan of giving away all assets and then waiting three years is certainly allowed under the law, but this is a "brute force" approach to the problem. There's no finesse. It is a drastic step to take and fraught with peril. Once the money is transferred, a completed gift is made. The child becomes the legal owner of the money and with all of the obvious "what ifs."

What if the child goes bankrupt or dies?

What if the child is sued? Will a Court order the child to use the money you gave to pay the judgment?

What if the child is divorced? Will the Court decide that your child's spouse is entitled to half of that money?

But the real problem is the loss of independence. Being impoverished at a time in your life when you are unable to supplement your income, and when your physical health is declining, can lead to much sadness. Imagine going to your child and asking for money. Imagine the child thinking, or worse yet, asking
"What's the money for?"

And what if you give the money away and never need nursing care? Medical technology is advancing with amazing speed. Although few cures have been found for mankind's ills, there have been many breakthroughs in their treatment. With modern drugs, many patients are now able to function without the need for long-term care. Even those who have been diagnosed with a progressive disease may not need nursing care for several years — maybe never.

Meanwhile, the money is gone, and your independence along with it.

THE LONG RANGE QUALIFYING PLAN

Giving away all one's money and then waiting three years works, but at the cost of your independence. Putting money into an irrevocable Trust and waiting 5 years has its risks. A lot can happen in 5 years. You could require full nursing care the day after you transfer your assets into the Trust. Maybe the 5 year look-back is changed to a 6 year look back period.

For those in good health, an alternative is to do nothing until you actually need nursing home care and then implement a Medical Assistance Qualifying strategy at that time. Of course there is the chance that you take suddenly ill, say with a stroke, and are too ill to put a plan into effect plan. But a properly drafted Durable Power Of Attorney should solve the problem. You can appoint your spouse or child to be your Agent to do so for you.

It is important that the Durable Power of Attorney be properly drafted. In December, 2002, A New Jersey Court refused to allow a son to transfer property on behalf of his incapacitated mother for purpose of qualifying for Medicaid. Although his mother gave him a Power of Attorney authorizing him to apply for Medicaid on her behalf, the Court refused to allow the transfer because the Power of Attorney ". . . did not provide for him to make gifts on her behalf to himself or anyone else, either to qualify her for Medicaid or for any other reason" (*In the Matter of Mildred Keri*, Superior Court of New Jersey, Appellate Division, A-5949-01T5).

Courts in this state might take a similar approach, so those who are concerned about qualifying for Medical Assistance need to have their attorney draft a Durable Power of Attorney giving their Agent specific authority to implement a Medical Assistance Qualifying plan.

CAUTION: THE ONLY THING CERTAIN IS CHANGE

The discussion relating to Medical Assistance Programs Qualifying Plans for the state of Pennsylvania is not intended to lull the reader into a false sense of security. The only thing certain about federal and state laws is that they will change. Whatever strategy you choose may not be around when you need it.

For example, we explained how a Community Spouse with too much in Resources and too little income is allowed to keep as much of those excess Resources as is necessary to get her to the Minimum Need Allowance. Legislators are considering changing that rule so that the Community Spouse must first use as much of the Recipient's income to get her to that Minimum Need Allowance. She will not be allowed to keep extra Resources unless the combination of her income and her spouse's income is not equal to the Minium Need Allowance as determined by CAO.

In addition to changes in the Pennsylvania law, the federal government is considering giving states new powers to control the Medical Assistance program within their state. Under this proposal, benefits for welfare recipients, poor children and other groups who are automatically eligible for Medical Assistance Programs would remain regulated by federal law. The state would be given autonomy to administer Medical Assistance Programs for other groups; and in particular for the elderly in need of nursing care. If this plan is implemented, it will be up to the state to decide whether to reduce, eliminate or increase Medical Assistance Program benefits for the elderly within the given state.

Proponents of state autonomy explain that with autonomy, the state could increase benefits, but in these days of budget deficits, more likely the states will opt to decrease Medical Assistance Program benefits to the elderly.

And that is not the only problem with the proposed plan. If states are given autonomy in administering the long-term nursing care program, there would no longer be uniformity imposed by current federal statutes. Medical Assistance Programs for the elderly could vary significantly state to state. Not only would there be variation state to state, but there could be variation within the state. State programs could be administered with different eligibility criteria county to county. There could even be a difference in benefits county to county. The point is that there is no certainty when it comes to future Medical Assistance qualifying options.

But we did not write this chapter to give the reader a definitive Medical Assistance Qualifying strategy. Rather it was to give the reader an understanding of the law as it relates to qualifying for Medical Assistance Programs; and to let the reader know that under current law, options are available should the need for long-term nursing care arise in the future. We also wrote this chapter to let the general public understand how this federal program is administered here in the state of Pennsylvania.

Incidentally, we touched only on the basics. There are other, more sophisticated, Medical Assistance Qualifying options available that an experienced Elder Law attorney can explain to you.

The prudent thing to do is to visit an Elder Law attorney if and when you become concerned about a long term care problem. He can explain current law to you as it relates to qualifying for Medical Assistance Programs. He can suggest the best path for you to follow, given your set of circumstances.

It is also important to keep up with changes in policy both in the state and federal government; and to let your legislators know how you feel about such changes.

Protecting the Homestead   11

We discussed the problem of having cash assets in excess of that allowed under current federal and state law; but what about the person whose only asset of value is his home? As explained in Chapter 10, whether the home counts as a Resource for purposes of qualifying for Medical Assistance depends on whether the Applicant has expressed an intent to return home. If the Applicant intends to return to his home, regardless of the value of the home, he will not be denied Medical Assistance benefits because he owns his home. However, if the Recipient has not expressed an intent to return home, the state can place a *Medicaid Lien*** on the property for monies spent on his behalf. When the property is sold, the state will be reimbursed from the sale proceeds.

Even if the state does not place a lien on his home during his lifetime, if the Medical Assistance Recipient received public medical assistance after the age of 55, the state has the right to place a Medicaid Lien on his home once he dies. The state will not place a lien on the home of a Medical Assistance Recipient while his spouse and/or minor or disabled child are living in his home. However, once the minor child reaches 21, or the spouse and disabled child are deceased, whoever inherits the home of the Medical Assistance Recipient will need to pay off that lien or the state can force the sale of the property and take the money from the proceeds of the sale of the house (42 U.S.C.A. 1396a(1)(B), 42 CFR 433.36).

**As explained, *Medicaid* is included as part of Pennsylvania's *Medical Assistance Programs*. We have used the terms interchangeably.

213

Of course the simple solution for a married Applicant is to transfer title to the homestead to his spouse. Under state and federal law, he can do so at any time, without penalty (42 U.S.C. 1396p (c)2(A), 55 Pa.Code 178.104). If the property is in the Applicant's name only, he can sign a deed conveying the property to his spouse. If they own the property jointly, they both can sign a deed transferring the property to the Community Spouse.

It is more of a problem for the aged, single parent; and it is a problem for aging parents who both are not in the best of health. Who knows which of them will require long term nursing care? Maybe both will need such care. Maybe neither of them will require nursing care.

Most parents want to have their children inherit the one thing the parent has of value, namely their home. Parents fear that if they ever need Medical Assistance benefits, their home will be sold to reimburse the state. This idea is so distressing to some parents that even though they are in relatively good health, they may decide to transfer their home to their child with the understanding that the parents will continue to live there for the rest of their lives.

Those planning such a move need to understand that they are trading one risk (the need to apply for Medical Assistance) for several other risks.

☒ RISK OF LOSS

Once you transfer the property to your child it becomes his property and that property can be lost or used to pay for his debts just like anything else he owns. Your child could run into serious financial difficulties. Your child could be sued. This is especially a risk if your child is a professional (doctor, nurse, accountant, financial planner, attorney, etc.). If your child is found to be personally liable for damages, then your home could become part of the settlement of that law suit.

If your child is (or gets) married, then this complicates matters even more. If the child divorces, the value of your home might be included as part of the property settlement agreement. This may be to your child's detriment because the child may need to share the value of the property with his/her ex-spouse. If you do not transfer the property, it cannot become part of his marital equation. Once divorced, your child could be sued for back child or spouse support. A Court could order that your house be sold to pay for monies he owes.

Even if your child is single, there is a risk of loss. Your child may want to take out a business loan. It the loan is significant, the lender will want to include everything your child owns as collateral (security for the debt). If the lender learns that you are occupying the house, he will especially want to include your house as collateral because that will motivate your son to repay the loan.

The point is, that transferring your home to your child could be bad for both of you. And that is not the only downside.

☒ **POSSIBLE CAPITAL GAINS TAX**

Although Congress has expressed its intent to phase out the Estate Tax, there is no discussion to do away with the Capital Gains Tax. If you gift the property to the child during your lifetime, when he sells the property he will pay a Capital Gains Tax on the increase in value from the price you paid for your home to the selling price at the time your child sells the property.

If you do not make the gift during your lifetime, the child will inherit the property with a step-up in basis, i.e., he will inherit the property at its market value as of the date of your death. Under today's tax structure and continuing until 2009, that step-up in basis is unlimited. If your child sells the property when he inherits it, he will pay no Capital Gains Tax, regardless of how large the step-up in basis.

In 2010, there will be a limit on the amount that can be inherited free of the Capital Gains Tax but that limit is quite high so for most of us this is not a concern.

☒ **POSSIBLE GIFT TAX**

A Gift Tax needs to be paid if the value of the equity in your home (plus the value of all the gifts you gave over your lifetime in excess of Annual Gift Tax Exclusion) exceeds the Gift Tax Exclusion. The current Exclusion is $1,000,000, so for most of us, this is not a problem. Yet, there still is the hassle of filing a Gift Tax return.

⊠ POSSIBLE LOSS OF GOVERNMENT BENEFITS

If you are married and you transfer property to someone other than your spouse, then depending upon the value of the transfer, both you and your spouse could be disqualified from receiving Medicaid or Supplemental Security Income ("SSI") if you apply within 3 years from the date of transfer of the property. That increases to 5 years if you transfer the property into a Trust.

It could happen that during that period of time, one of you takes suddenly ill and requires long-term nursing care.

Why jeopardize your right to receive Medical Assistance for both of you? Owning a homestead will not disqualify you from receiving Medical Assistance, but transferring it may make you and your spouse ineligible for a long time.

The elderly parent, who is single, may not be convinced that gifting the house is a bad idea. He may argue "By giving my home to my child, I risk not being able to qualify for Medical Assistance for three years. If I don't make the gift and need Medical Assistance at any time during the rest of my lifetime, the state will get the house for sure."

But there are better Estate Plans than the outright gift. The Life Estate strategy is one of them.

THE LIFE ESTATE STRATEGY

You can give the property to your child, and keep a Life Estate for yourself. Your child will have no right to your homestead while you are alive so you have no fear that the property can be lost or taken from you during your lifetime. Upon your death, your child will own the property 100%, and without the need for Probate. If you receive Medical Assistance benefits at any time during your life, there can be no recovery from the homestead because all you kept was the right to continue to live in the home during your life time.

Depending on the value of your home, this Life Estate approach might allow you to shorten the Medical Assistance transfer penalty period, because you are not giving your child the full value of your home, you are just giving away the value of the Remainder Interest i.e., what is left of the property after your death.

The value of the Remainder Interest depends on your life expectancy. A gift of a Remainder Interest when you are 90 is worth more to your child than when you are 50.

DETERMINING THE VALUE OF THE REMAINDER INTEREST

The Centers for Medicare and Medicaid Services publishes a table of values for the Life Estate Interest and the Remainder Interest based on the age of the Grantor at the time of the transfer (State Medicaid Manual, Part 3 (SM3 3258.9) LIFE ESTATE AND REMAINDER INTEREST TABLE). You can find excerpts from this table, at the author's Web site: http://www.fantinilaw.com

Fortunately, this table goes up to age 109, so the value they assign to the remainder interest is relatively low. For example, according to this table, if a 70 year old makes a transfer to his son and keeps a Life Estate for himself, his Life Estate is equal to 61% of the value of the property. The remainder interest is worth only 39%.

The actual percentage given in the table for the Remainder Interest is .39478. If the home is worth $100,000 it means the value of the gift of the Remainder Interest is $39,478. This greatly reduces the penalty period. If you transferred the house and did not keep a Life Estate, your penalty period would be 18 months:
$$\$100,000/\$5,313.18 = 18 \text{ months}$$

By keeping a Life Estate that penalty period significantly reduces that penalty period:
$$\$39,478/\$5,313.18 = 7 \text{ months.}$$

A Life Estate is a better Medicaid Qualifying Plan than an outright gift but it is not a complete solution because you are still making a lifetime gift. Issues of control and taxes still remain. You will not be able to sell your home without permission from your child. And, as explained at the end of Chapter 2, if you sell the home, you might need to pay a Capital Gains tax.

Before you decide to transfer your home to your child and keep a Life Estate for yourself, it is important to investigate the full tax consequence of the transfer; and then check with an Elder Law attorney to determine the Penalty Period that will be imposed because of the transfer.

TRANSFERS THAT PROTECT

As explained, under state and federal law, a married Applicant can protect his home from a Medicaid Lien by transferring the property to his spouse. The Applicant is free to transfer his home to his spouse either before or after he qualifies for Medical Assistance. Should the Applicant be too ill to make the transfer himself, the deed can be signed by his Agent under a properly drafted Durable Power of Attorney. If he does not have a Power of Attorney, and is too ill to sign his name, it may be necessary to have a Guardian appointed who can ask the Court for permission to make the transfer.

Going through a guardianship procedure may be expensive and time consuming, but it is important that the homestead be transferred to the Community spouse because it could happen that the Community spouse dies first leaving the home in the name of the now single Medical Assistance Recipient.

The downside is that there is no guarantee that the judge will allow the transfer of the homestead to the Community Spouse. Before you apply for guardianship it is important to ask your attorney whether such transfers have been allowed in the past.

The single Applicant may be able to protect his home from a Medicaid Lien by transferring it to a child or sibling.

TRANSFERRING THE HOME TO A SIBLING

Under state and federal law, if an Applicant owns his home together with a sibling and the sibling lived with the Applicant for at least one year before entering the nursing facility, then the Applicant can transfer the home to the sibling without a Medical Assistance transfer penalty (42 U.S.C. 1396p, 55 Pa.Code 178.104). This law presents an opportunity for an unmarried Applicant who has a brother or sister to protect the homestead. The only question is how the sibling becomes co-owner. If the Applicant and his sibling purchased the property together, and the sibling lived in the home for a year prior to the Applicant entering the nursing home, then the sibling's interest in the property is protected. The Applicant can transfer his share of the homestead to his sibling without penalty, and that will protect all of the homestead.

If the house is in the Applicant's name only, then it is important to consult with an Elder Law attorney to determine the best way for the sibling to become part owner of the home. Federal law only requires that the sibling have an *equity interest* in the property. An equity interest could be joint ownership or a Tenancy-In-Common or a Remainder Interest in the homestead. An Elder Law attorney will be able to suggest a method of transferring an equity interest to the sibling that will result in a penalty period of a year or less. The attorney will also assist with preparing documentation to present to CAO (the County Assistance Office) to verify that:
- ⇨ the sibling owns an equity interest in the home
- ⇨ the penalty period for the transfer has passed
- ⇨ the sibling occupied the home for a year prior to the Applicant entering the nursing home.

TRANSFERRING THE HOME TO A CHILD

In Pennsylvania, the Applicant or his spouse may transfer their home, or any of their other assets to a child (minor or adult) who is blind, or disabled without penalty, provided the transfer is for the sole benefit of the disabled child (42 U.S.C. 1396p(c)(2A), 55 Pa.Code 178.104).

In the event that the child does not have a determination of blindness or disability from the Social Security Administration, the CAO will review the child's medical records to determine whether the child is blind or disabled.

If the child is receiving Social Security disability benefits, the parent can transfer money to a Special Needs Trust for the child (see Chapter 7). This transfer will not disqualify the child (or the parent) from receiving government benefits, provided the Trust is drafted according to state and federal law. It is important that an experienced Elder Law attorney draft the Trust and clear it with CAO prior to funding the Trust.

TRANSFER TO A CAREGIVER CHILD

Federal law allows a transfer of the Applicant's home to a child who is not disabled, provided the child lived with and took care of his parent for at least two years before the parent entered the nursing home (55 Pa.Code 178.104).

There is no requirement that the child own an equity interest in the property; but the federal statute does require that the state verify that the child lived in the home and provided care to the parent for the two years; and that this care enabled the parent to remain at home rather than be placed in a nursing home (42 U.S.C. 1396p(c)(2)(A)(iv)).

Of course, if the value of the house is not greater than the two year penalty period it may be just as easy to transfer the home to the child and wait out the two years. Specifically, a transfer of $127,516.32 will result in a 2 year penalty period: $5,313.18 x 24 = $127,516.32

If the parent's equity in the home is worth no more than $127,516.32, the home can be transferred to the child without the need for the child to prove to CAO that care was given to the parent over that two year period.

If the home is worth significantly more, then it is important to consult with an Elder Law attorney, preferably prior to the two year period. The attorney will explain how to document that care over the two year period so that the information can be presented to the CAO when the parent applies for Medical Assistance.

Some of the things the CAO will want to see are:

A physician's Affidavit stating that:

⇨ the parent needed continuous nursing care during the two year period prior to being placed in a nursing home

⇨ The parent would have needed institutional nursing care during that two year period had the child not provided such care at home.

The child's Affidavit stating that:

⇨ the child lived with the parent for the two years immediately prior to the parent entering the nursing home.

⇨ the care provided by the child enabled the parent to remain at home during those two years rather than being placed in a nursing home.

Once it is established by the CAO that state and federal requirements are satisfied, the property can be transferred to the child without affecting the right of the Applicant to receive Medical Assistance benefits.

CAUTION DON'T TRY THIS ON YOUR OWN

The strategies we have discussed in Chapters 10 and 11 are not something to attempt on your own. The Medicaid program is complex and volatile. There are four levels of laws that govern Pennsylvania's Medical Assistance Program. There are the federal statutes (Social Security Act Title XIX/P.L. 89-97); and the U.S. Code of Federal Regulations (42 CFR 430-435) that says how the federal statutes are to be administered in the United States. There are the Pennsylvania Medical Assistance statutes (Titles 62 and 67); and the Pennsylvania Code of Regulations (Title 55) that says how the Medical Assistance program is to be administered in Pennsylvania.

That's four levels of rules and regulations that are constantly changing — often with little or no notice to the general public. And the laws are not well written. This is what judges in federal courts have said about Medcaid statutes:

"The Social Security Act is among the most intricate ever drafted by Congress. Its Byzantine construction ... makes the Act 'almost intelligible to the uninitiated. ... The District Court ... described the Medicaid statute as 'an aggravated assault on the English language, resistant to attempts to understand it'." *Schweiker v. Gray Panthers*, 453 U.S. 34(1981).

In *Rehabilitation Association of Virginia v. Kozlowski*, 42 F.3d 1444, 1450 (4th Cir 1994), the Court had nothing but sympathy for officials who must interpret or administer the Act. "There can be no doubt that the statutes and provisions in question, involving the financing of Medicare and Medicaid, are among the most impenetrable texts within human experience. Indeed, one approaches them ... with dread, for not only are they dense reading of the most tortuous kind, but Congress also revisits the area frequently, generously cutting and pruning in the process and making any solid grasp of the matters addressed merely a passing phase."

Most states have a manual that is given to workers who are in charge of implementing the Medicaid Program. In Pennsylvania, that manual is the **INTAKE WORKER'S NURSING HOME HANDBOOK**. The Handbook explains how the Intake Worker is to apply the state's statutes and regulations; and in particular, how to determine eligibility for the state's Medical Assistance Programs. The Manual is not available on the Internet, but copies can be obtained by writing to the Pennsylvania Department of Public Welfare. Even with the Manual available to the Intake Workers, there is variation in the way the law is applied. What may be an acceptable Medicaid Qualifying option in one county, may be challenged by the CAO in another county. If the CAO decides to challenge a particular strategy, even though that strategy is based on federal or state law, you will have no choice but to appeal the ruling.

THE MEDICAID APPEAL

An Applicant who is denied Medical Assistance benefits will receive notice from CAO that he has the right to appeal. The first step in the appeal process is for the Applicant, or someone acting on his behalf, to request a "Fair Hearing." Once requested, the CAO will review the case to verify that the decision in question was made according to Department regulations. If Department regulations were followed, they will forward a letter requesting an appeal to the Bureau of Hearings and Appeals. The Bureau will appoint a qualified agency officer who was not involved in the denial of benefits, to serve as the Administrative Law Judge (55 Pa.Code 275.1, 55 Pa.Code 275.4).

The Administrative Law Judge will conduct the hearing and decide the matter. Although the hearing is conducted in an informal manner, it is, none-the-less, a complex legal proceeding. The CAO will prepare their case; and if they wish they will be assisted by an attorney from the Office of the Legal Counsel of the Department of Public Welfare. The attorney will present evidence and quote laws that support the ruling of the CAO.

To win you will need to have a complete understanding of all applicable law. You will need to know how to discover and present evidence to prove your case. Regardless of whether the CAO elects to be represented by an attorney, it is important that you have your own attorney to represent you. If you cannot afford to employ an attorney, then ask your local Legal Aid office for assistance.

The Administrative Law Judge will base his decision on the issue of whether the CAO applied the regulations correctly. More likely than not he will find that they did follow regulations. The Administrative Law Judge will send his report and ruling to the Director of the Bureau of Hearings and Appeals. The Director will review the case. If he agrees with the decision of the Administrative Law Judge, and denys the appeal, the Applicant may, within 15 days of the Director's decision, ask that the Secretary of the Department of Public Welfare reconsider his decision (55 Pa.Code 275.4).

If the Applicant loses at this administrative level, he can take the case before the Commonwealth Court. The Court will take a broader look at the picture and consider state and federal law, as well as the Constitutional rights of the Applicant. If the Applicant is turned down at the state level, he can appeal to a federal court — all the way up to the United States Supreme Court.

As you can see, appealing the CAO's decision is complicated, and time consuming. It is important to employ an attorney to help with the appeal and that can be expensive. He may recommend that you skip the Administrative Appeal process altogether and bring your case directly to the Commonwealth Court.

Of course, the best approach is to try to avoid the need for an appeal in the first place. In Chapter 10 we presented many different options that are legally available to the Applicant at this time. The goal is to get the Applicant qualified for Medical Assistance as quickly as possible, and with the least amount of hassle. It is better to choose a strategy that has been allowed in the past, rather than chance a denial of the application and be forced to appeal the decision.

An experienced Elder Law attorney can explain what strategies have been allowed in the past in your county and which strategies are likely to be challenged. The key word is "experienced." Before employing an attorney, determine what percentage of his practice is devoted to Medical Assistance eligibility; how long he has practiced Elder Law in that county; and whether he is familiar with the appeals process, should the need arise.

Guiding Those You Love 12

Once you are satisfied with your Estate Plan, then the final thing to consider is whether your heirs will be able to locate your assets after you're gone.

Most people have their business records in one place, their Will in another place, car titles and deeds in still another place. When someone dies, their beneficiaries may feel as if they are playing a game of "hide and seek" with the decedent. The game might be fun were it not for the fact that unlocated items may be forever lost. For example, suppose you die in an accident and no one knows you are insured by your credit card company for accidental death in the amount of $25,000. The only one to profit is the insurance company, which is just that much richer because no one told them that you died as a result of an accident.

And how about a key to a safe deposit box? Will anyone find it? Even if they find the key, how will they locate the box?

It is not difficult to arrange things so that your affairs are always in order. It amounts to being aware of what you own (and owe) and keeping a record of your possessions. A side benefit is that by doing so, you will always know where all your business records are. If you ever spent time trying to collect information to file your taxes or trying to find a lost stock or bond certificate, you will appreciate the value of organizing your records.

POINTING THE WAY

Heirs need all the help they can get. It is difficult enough dealing with the loss, without the frustration of trying to locate important documents. Your heirs will have no problem locating your assets if you keep all of your records in a single place. It can be a desk drawer or a file cabinet or even a shoe box. It is helpful if you keep a separate file or folder for each type of investment. You might consider setting up the following folders:

📁 THE BANK & SECURITIES FOLDER

Store your original certificates for stocks, bonds, mutual funds, certificates of deposit, in a folder labeled BANK & SECURITIES FOLDER. In addition to the original certificate include a copy of the contract you signed with each financial institution. The contract will show where you have funds and who you named as beneficiary or joint owner of the account. If someone owes you money and has signed a promissory note or mortgage that identifies you as the lender, then you can store these documents in this folder as well.

If you wish to store your original documents in a safe deposit box, then keep a record of the location of the safe deposit box, and the number of the box, in this folder. Make a copy of all of the items stored in the box and place the copies in this folder. If you have an extra key to the box, then put the key in the folder. If you are the only person with access to the box, it may take a Probate procedure to remove items from the box once you die. Consider giving someone you trust the right to gain entry to the box in the event of your incapacity or death.

📁 THE INSURANCE FOLDER

The **INSURANCE FOLDER** is for each original insurance policy that you own, be it car insurance, homeowner's insurance or a health care insurance policy. If you purchased real property, you may have received a title commitment at closing and the original title insurance policy some weeks later when you received your original deed from the Recorder's Office. If you cannot locate the title insurance policy, then contact the closing agent and have them send you a copy of your title insurance policy.

📁 THE PENSION AND ANNUITY FOLDER

Put all of the documents relating to your pension or annuity in this folder. Include the telephone number and/or address of the person to contact in the event of your death.

FOR FEDERAL RETIREES

If you are a Federal Retiree, you should have received your **PERSONAL IDENTIFICATION NUMBER** (**PIN**) and the person who will inherit your pension (your *survivor annuitant*) should have received his/her own **PIN** as well. It is relatively simple to obtain this during your lifetime, but it may be difficult and/or stressful for your survivor annuitant to work through the system once you are gone.

Survivor annuitant benefits are not automatic. Your survivor annuitant must apply for them by submitting a death claim to the Office of Personnel Management. Your survivor needs to know that it is necessary to apply and also how to apply. You can call the Office of Personnel Management at (888) 767-6738 to get printed information that you can keep in this folder to guide your survivor annuitant through the process.

📁 THE DEED FOLDER

Many people save every scrap of paper associated with the closing of real property. If you closed recently on real estate and there was a mortgage involved in the purchase, you probably walked away from closing with enough paper to wallpaper your kitchen. If you wish, you can keep all of those papers in a separate file that identifies the property, for example:

> CLOSING PAPERS FOR THE PITTSBURGH PROPERTY

Place the original deed (or a copy if the original is in a safe deposit box) in a separate **DEED FOLDER**. Include cemetery deeds, condominium deeds, timesharing certificates, deed to out of state property, etc. Also include a copy of related documents such as an Abstract of Title, or a recorded condominium approval. If you have a title insurance policy, put the original in the insurance folder, and a copy in this folder. If you have a mortgage on your property, put a copy of the recorded mortgage and promissory note in a separate **LIABILITY FOLDER**.

Once the mortgage is paid off, the lender should give you a Satisfaction of Mortgage. The Satisfaction needs to be recorded. You can keep the recorded Satisfaction together with the deed to the property.

LOCATING REAL PROPERTY

If you own a vacant lot, your beneficiaries will find the deed (or a copy) in this folder but that deed will not contain the address of that property because it doesn't have one. The post office does not assign a street address until there is a building on the site. Your beneficiary could get the location of the property from city or county records. But why make things hard for them? Include a simple handwritten note in this folder that tells them exactly how to locate the property.

📁 THE TAX RECORD FOLDER

Your Personal Representative (or next of kin) will need to file your final income tax returns. Keep a copy of your tax returns (both federal and state) for the past three years in your Tax Record folder. As explained in Chapter 3, beginning in 2010, there will be a cap on the step-up basis to 4.3 million dollars for property inherited by your spouse and 1.3 million for property inherited by anyone else. It is important to keep a record of the basis of your property, not only for your heirs, but for yourself should you decide to sell the property during your lifetime. If you purchase real property, you need to keep a record of the purchase price as well as monies you paid to improve the property. You need these records to determine whether a Capital Gains Tax is due on the transfer. Your accountant can help you set up a bookkeeping system to keep a running record of your basis in everything you own of value.

📁 THE LIABILITY FOLDER

The LIABILITY FOLDER should contain all loan documents of debts that you owe. For example, if you purchased real property and have a mortgage on that property, put a copy of the mortgage and promissory note in this folder. If you owe money on a car, put the loan documents in this folder. A lease is a liability, because you have contracted to pay a certain amount for the period of the lease, so include a copy of any lease agreement in this folder.

If you have a credit card, put a copy of the contract you signed with the credit card company in this folder. Many people never take the time to calculate their net worth (what a person owns less what that person owes). By having a record of your assets and outstanding debts, you can calculate your net worth whenever you wish.

📁 THE PERSONAL PROPERTY FOLDER

MOTOR VEHICLES
Put all motor vehicle titles in a Personal Property folder. This includes cars, mobile homes, boats, planes, etc. If you owe money on the vehicle, the lender may have possession of the title certificate. If such is the case, then put a copy of the title certificate and registration in this folder and a copy of the loan documents in a separate liability folder. If you own a boat or plane, then identify the location of the motor vehicle. For example, if you are leasing space in an airplane hangar or in a marina, keep a copy of the leasing agreement in this folder.

JEWELRY
If you own expensive jewelry, keep a picture of the item together with the sales receipt or written appraisal in this folder.

COLLECTOR'S ITEMS
If you own a valuable art or coin collection, or any other item of significant value, include a picture of the item in this folder. Also include evidence of ownership of the item, such as a sales receipt or a certificate of authenticity, or a written appraisal of the property.

📁 THE PERSONAL RECORDS FOLDER

The PERSONAL RECORDS FOLDER should include documents that relate to you personally, such as a birth certificate, naturalization papers, marriage certificate, divorce papers, military records, social security card; etc.

📁 THE ESTATE PLANNING DOCUMENT FOLDER

WILL/TRUST

Place your Will and/or Trust in a separate folder. If the original document is in a safe deposit box, then place a copy of the document in this folder together with instructions about how to find the original. If your attorney has your original Will, then make a note of that fact together with a copy of the Will.

It is important to keep a copy of your Will or Trust because over the years you may forget what provision you made. Keeping a copy in your home may save you the time and effort to retrieve the document, just to determine whether it needs to be updated.

PRENUPTIAL/POSTNUPTIAL AGREEMENT

Prenuptial or postnuptial agreements usually provide for the disposition of your property upon your death, so a copy of the agreement should be included in this folder.

OTHER ESTATE PLANNING DOCUMENTS

You can include the original or a copy of your Power of Attorney, Medical Directive or Preneed Funeral Plan in this folder.

THE QUICK-FIND FOLDER

Many do not have the time, nor inclination, to "play" with all these folders. They do not anticipate an immediate demise. Getting hit by a truck, or dying in a fiery plane crash is not something to think about, much less prepare for. But consider that death is not the only problem. You could take suddenly ill (say with a stroke) and become incapacitated. Even the most time-starved optimist should have a murmur of concern that his loved ones will be left with a mess should something unforeseen happen.

If you do not feel like doing a complete job of organizing your records at this time, consider an abridged version. You can set up a single folder and place all of your important papers in that folder. You need to make the folder easily accessible to whoever you wish to manage your affairs in the event of your incapacity or death. You can do this by letting that person know of the existence of the folder and how to get it in an emergency.

You can keep the folder in an easily accessed place in your home with the folder identified as containing important papers. We labeled it "THE QUICK-FIND FOLDER" because the folder gives you and your family easy access to important information and/or documents. But you can create your own heading such as: "MY IMPORTANT PAPERS" or if you want a particular person to access the folder, you might label it: "RECORDS FOR MY SON, ROBERT"

It is helpful if you include a list of all you own and the location of each item in that folder. There is a form that you can use on the next page to assist with your organization of your important papers.

THE QUICK FIND FOLDER

FINANCIAL RECORDS

BANK
Name and address of Bank, Account Number,
_____
_____

Location of Safe Deposit Box and Key
_____

SECURITIES
Identity and location of stocks and bonds:
_____
_____

Name, Telephone number of securities broker
_____

INSURANCE POLICIES

Name of Company, Location of Policy, Insurance Agent
_____
_____

PENSIONS/ANNUITIES

_____
NAME OF CONTACT PERSON _____

IF FEDERAL RETIREE: PIN NUMBER: _____

TAX RECORDS

LOCATION_____
Name, Telephone number of accountant
_____

PROPERTY RECORDS

TITLE TO MOTOR VEHICLES _____
DEEDS _____
MORTGAGES _____

LIABILITY RECORD

MORTGAGES_____
LEASES _____
PROMISSORY NOTES_____
CREDIT CARDS _____

LOCATION OF LEGAL DOCUMENTS

BIRTH CERTIFICATE AND/OR NATURALIZATION PAPERS

_____

PASSPORT _____
MARRIAGE CERTIFICATE _____
DIVORCE DECREE _____

ARMED SERVICE DISCHARGE PAPERS

_____

LOCATION OF ESTATE PLANNING DOCUMENTS

WILL _____

TRUST _____

PRENUPTIAL/POSTNUPTIAL AGREEMENT

_____

PATIENT ADVOCATE DESIGNATION _____

POWER OF ATTORNEY _____

PRENEED FUNERAL PLAN _____

ATTORNEY
Name, Telephone number _____

_____

WHEN TO UPDATE YOUR ESTATE PLAN

We discussed people's natural disinclination to make an Estate Plan until they are faced with their own mortality. Many believe that they will make just one Will and then die (maybe that's why they put off making a Will). The reality is, most people who make a Will change it at least once before they die. If you have an Estate Plan, it is important to update it when any of the following events take place:

✎ **CHANGE IN MARITAL STATUS**

If you marry or divorce, there are certain changes that take place by law. For example, if you divorce and die before you get around to changing your Will, any provision that you made for your ex-spouse in the document will no longer be effective (20 Pa.C.S. 6111.1). Property you own together as a Tenancy By The Entirety becomes a Tenancy-In-Common with you and your "Ex" each owning half of the property (23 Pa.C.S.A. 3507).

If you named your spouse as the beneficiary of your life insurance policy, the benefits will be paid in the same manner as if your former spouse died first. But it is important to not just rely on the law, because if the insurance company is not notified of the divorce and they pay the money to your former spouse, they will not be held liable for the error. Whoever is entitled to that money will have the job of getting it back from your former spouse (20 Pa.C.S. 6111.2).

To avoid such problems it is best to change all documents after a divorce or separation. This includes a Power of Attorney, Advance Directive For Health Care, deed, bank account, etc.

NOTIFY EMPLOYER OF CHANGE

If you change your marital status (either marry or divorce) you need to tell your employer of the change so that the employer can change your status for purposes of paycheck tax deductions. If you have health insurance plan or a pension plan, that provides benefits to your spouse, then these need to be changed as well.

Pennsylvania law allows up to $5,000 in wages to be transferred to your spouse upon your death. If you change your marital status, then tell your employer, in writing, who is to receive your unpaid wages in the event of your death, and ask your employer to put that document in your work file. If no designation is made, then under Pennsylvania law, the money goes to a family member in the following order of priority: child, parent, brother or sister (20 Pa.C.S. 3101).

✍ A CHANGE IN RELATIONSHIP

Getting married, separated or divorced; having a child; having a beneficiary of your Estate die, these are all profound changes in one's life. When the dust settles, it is important to examine your Estate Plan to see if it needs revision. If you have a Trust you can change it by having your attorney prepare an amendment to the Trust. You can change your Will by adding a *codicil* (a supplement) to the Will. If you decide that your Will needs a complete revision, then it is important to have a new Will prepared. If you simply rip up the old Will, that will effectively revoke the Will (20 Pa.C.S. 2505). But it could happen that someone (perhaps your attorney) has a copy of the Will. If no one knows that you revoked the Will, they may think the Will is lost and then offer the copy of the Will for Probate. If you draft a new Will, then the first paragraph should say, "I revoke all prior Wills ..." This makes it clear that you want the new Will to replace all other Wills.

CAUTION   NEW SPOUSE OR CHILD CAN
                     CHALLENGE OLD WILL

CHALLENGE BY SURVIVING SPOUSE

If you marry and "forget" to change the Will you prepared prior to your marriage, then your spouse can challenge your Will and ask the Court to be given as much as he/she would have received had you died without a Will. Under Pennsylania law, your spouse is entitled to the intestate share unless it appears that you prepared the Will in contemplation of your upcoming marriage, or unless your spouse signed a prenuptial or postnuptial agreement giving up the right to inherit an intestate share (20 Pa.C.S.A. 2507).

CHALLENGE BY AFTERBORN CHILD

Similarly, a child born or adopted after you prepared your Will is entitled to a share of your Probate Estate, unless your Will makes it clear that you intentionally made no provision for the child. In the absence of such provision, the child is entitled to as much as he/she would have received had you died without a Will, not including that part of your Probate Estate inherited by your surviving spouse.

If you left all of your property to your surviving spouse, it could be that your child gets nothing. If you are not married and your child is your only heir, it could be that your child gets everything and the beneficiaries named in your Will get nothing. It is better that you change your Will when a child is born so that your child receives no more and no less than you intended.

✍ BENEFICIARY MOVES OR DIES

Most people remember to name an alternate beneficiary should one of their beneficiaries die. But how many of us remember to notify the insurance company or our pension plan when a beneficiary moves?

It is important that your beneficiary's address be available to those in charge of distributing funds upon your death. Many life insurance proceeds are never paid because the company cannot locate the beneficiary. The Actuarial Office of the Federal Employees' Group Life Insurance Program reported that as of October, 2001, they had over 40 million dollars in unpaid benefits, mostly because they could not locate the beneficiary at the last given address.

✍ RELOCATION TO A NEW STATE OR COUNTRY

There is no need to change your Estate Plan for a move within the state of Pennsylvania. There is much to check out if you are moving to another state. If your attorney has your original Will or any other original of your Estate Planning documents, then you may want to retrieve these items and take them with you to the new state.

You need to determine whether your Will conforms to the laws of the state of your new residence. Most states will honor a Will drafted according to Pennsylvania law, however, the rights of a spouse vary considerably state to state. If you are married and have not provided the minimum amount as required by the laws of the new state, then should you die before your spouse, your Will may be challenged on that basis. The same applies to a Trust. Many states allow a surviving spouse to demand funds from the Trust of the decedent spouse, if the deceased spouse did not provide the minimum amount to his spouse as required by the laws of that state.

LAWS OF INTESTATE SUCCESSION

If you do not have a Will, then it is important to check out the Laws of Intestate Succession for that state. In some states they are referred to as the *Laws of Descent and Distribution* Each state has its own laws relating to the inheritance of property and those laws can be very different from each other. Who has the right to inherit your property in the Commonwealth of Pennsylvania may be different from who can inherit your property in another state. If you do not have a Will, then this is the time to think about who will get your property in the state of your new residence.

This is especially important for those who are married. The right of a spouse to inherit property varies significantly from state to state. There is a world of difference between the rights of a spouse in a community property state (Arizona, California, Idaho, Louisiana, Nevada, New Mexico, Texas, Washington and Wisconsin) and other states. There is even variation in the rights of a spouse from one community property state to another!

TAX CONSIDERATIONS

You need to check out the taxes of the new state. Each state has its own tax structure. Some states have an inheritance tax, or a transfer tax on all inherited property. If state taxes are high, you may need an Estate Plan that will minimize the impact of those taxes.

CREDITOR PROTECTION

Creditor protection is another item that is significantly different state to state. If you have much debt, then determine what items can be inherited by your family free of your debts.

OTHER ESTATE PLANNING DOCUMENTS

Many states have laws directing physicians to honor an Advance Directive for Health Care that is properly drafted in another state. Other states will not recognize a Medical Directive unless it is drafted according to the laws of that state. But even if the laws of the state honor your Pennsylvania Advance Directive for Health Care, consider drafting another in the new state. Medical Directives vary significantly state to state. Other states may have laws that enable you to appoint someone with powers similar to a Health Care Surrogate, but the laws of the state may refer to such person as a *Patient Advocate* or a *Health Care Agent* or a *Health Care Representative*.

It is best to sign a new Advance Directivefor Health Care using the form and terminology recognized in the new state, rather than chance any confusion should you become ill and find yourself in an emergency situation. Similarly, if you have appointed someone to handle your finances under a Power of Attorney, you may want to have another prepared in conformity with the laws of the new state, so there will be no question of the right of your Agent to conduct business on your behalf.

RELOCATING THE MEDICAID RECIPIENT

If a family member is Medicaid recipient, and you plan to move him to another state, you need to check out whether he will continue to be eligible for Medicaid in that state. As explained in the previous chapter, Medicaid is both a state and federal program. Once a person qualifies for Medicaid in one state, he can be transferred to another state; provided he qualifies under that state's Medical Assistance program.

For example, Pennsylvania does not have an upper limit for income, but other states do. If an Applicant has an income that exceeds the limit in a state that has an *income cap*, then the Applicant may be refused Medicaid benefits in that state.

If you plan to move a Medicaid recipient to another state, it is important to apply for Medicaid in that state and have a written acceptance into the Medicaid program before you make the move.

If the Medicaid Agency says that the recipient does not meet the state requirements for eligibility, then check with an Elder Law attorney to learn what options are available to allow the recipient to qualify for Medicaid in that state.

As you can see, state law has an important impact on your Estate Plan. When moving to another state, it is important to either educate yourself about the laws of the state, or to consult with an attorney who can assist you in reviewing your Estate Plan to see if that plan will accomplish your goals in that state.

✍ A SIGNIFICANT CHANGE IN THE LAW

We pay our legislators (state and federal) to make laws and, if necessary, change those in effect. We pay judges to interpret the law and that interpretation may change the way the law operates. The legislature and the judiciary do their job and so laws change frequently. Tax laws are particularly volatile. The 2001 change in the Federal Estate Tax law gradually increases the Exclusion amount so that by 2010 no Federal Estate Tax will be due regardless of the value of your Estate. You may be thinking that there is no need for an Estate Tax plan because you don't intend to die prior to 2010. But any certainty relating to death and taxes is false security (especially taxes, in this case). As explained in Chapter 2, the law as passed in 2001, is effective only until December 31, 2010. If lawmakers do nothing, then on January 1, 2011, the Federal Estate Tax goes back into effect; and Estates that exceed one million dollars will once again be subject to Estate taxes.

And that is not the only uncertainty. Each state has its own Estate Tax structure. It remains to be seen how each state will react to the federal change. Some states may follow the lead of the federal government and increase their Estate Tax Exclusion in the same manner. Other states may see this as an opportunity to "pick up the slack" i.e., to increase their Estate Taxes, so that monies that would have been paid to the federal government will now be paid to the state.

You need to keep up with the news to learn about changes in the law that affect your Estate Plan. It is a good idea to check with your attorney on a regular basis to see if any change in the state or federal law affects your current Estate plan. And also check out the Eagle Publishing Company Web site for changes we will post to keep this book fresh.   http://www.eaglepublishing.com

SPRING CLEANING YOUR RECORDS

Used to be, that housewives did a once a year, floor to ceiling, "spring housecleaning." We know of no survey telling whether today's houseperson conducts an annual purge of dirt and clutter. We suspect it went by the wayside when housewives entered the work force as full-time employees. But it was a good practice. In many cases, it was the only time of the year when the house was truly clean and tidy.

It is a good idea to incorporate that old-fashioned housecleaning practice to your financial records and clean them up on a regular basis. There is no need to keep the deed to real property that you have long since sold; a lease agreement to an apartment you no longer rent; a credit card to a closed account, etc.

Many hesitate to toss out some scrap of paper for fear it will not be available for future reference. There are documents you may need to keep for a lengthy period of time to establish a basis for tax purposes. You can avoid the problem of keeping too much, or not enough, by taking your box (or folder) of records with you the next time you visit with your accountant or attorney. You can ask your advisor to help you organize your records and assist with your "housecleaning."

Keys are another item to keep up to date. You may have a sentimental reason to keep old keys, but there is no business reason to keep a key to a car you no longer own, a safe deposit box you no longer lease, etc. Keeping such keys can only cause confusion should you become disabled or die. Whoever takes possession of your property will be left with mysterious keys. He will probably think the keys are protecting something of value.

Unless you enjoy picturing an heir's frustration as he seeks an imaginary treasure, pitch the key.

Glossary

ACTUARIAL TABLE An *actuarial table* is a table organized according to statistical data that indicates the life expectancy of a person.

ADMINISTRATION The *administration* of a Probate Estate is the management and settlement of the decedent's affairs. There are different types of administration.

ADVANCE DIRECTIVE An *Advance Directive for Health Care* is a writing made by someone (the *Declarant*) according to Pennsylvania law in which the Declarant gives specific instruction about the health care he wishes to receive in the event he is seriously ill and unable to speak for himself.

AFFIANT An *Affiant* is someone who signs an Affidavit and swears or acknowledges that it is true in the presence of a notary public or other person with authority to administer an oath or take acknowledgments.

AFFIDAVIT An *Affidavit* is a written statement of fact made by someone voluntarily, under oath, or acknowledged as being true, in the presence of a notary public or someone else who has authority to administer an oath or take acknowledgments.

AGENT An *Agent* is someone who is authorized by another (the principal) to act for, or in place of, the principal.

AMENDMENT An *amendment* to a Trust is an addition to the Trust that changes the provisions of the Trust.

ANATOMICAL GIFT   An *anatomical gift* is the donation of all or part of the body of the decedent for a specified purpose, such as transplantation or research.

ANNOTATED STATUTE A statute that is *annotated* is a statement of the statue followed by an illustration or explanation of that law.

ANNUITANT   An *Annuitant* is someone who is entitled to receive payments under an annuity contract.

ANNUITY CONTRACT An *annuity contract* is a contract that gives someone (the annuitant) the right to receive periodic payments (monthly, quarterly) for the life of the annuitant or for a given number of years.

ASSET   An *asset* is anything owned by someone that has a value, including personal property (jewelry, paintings, securities, cash, motor vehicles, etc.) and real property (condominiums, vacant lots, acreage, residences, etc.)

ASSIGNABLE   A pension is *assignable* if pensioner has the right to tranfer his right in the pension to another person.

ATTORNEY or ATTORNEY AT LAW   An *attorney*, also known as an *Attorney at law*, or a *lawyer*, is someone who is licensed by the state to practice law in that state.

ATTORNEY-IN-FACT An *Attorney-In-Fact* is someone appointed to act as an Agent for another (the Principal) under a Power of Attorney.

BASIS   The *basis* is a value that is assigned to an asset for the purpose of determining the gain (or loss) on the sale of the item or in determining the value of the item in the hands of someone who has received it as a gift.

BENEFICIARY A *beneficiary* is one who benefits from the act of another or from the transfer of property. In this book we refer to a beneficiary as someone named in a Will, Trust, or deed to receive property, or someone who inherits property under the Laws of Intestate Succession.

BY REPRESENTATION   *By Representation* is a method of distributing property to a group of people such that if one of them dies before the gift is made, the deceased person's share goes to his/her descendants.

CAPITAL GAINS TAX A *Capital Gains tax* is a tax on the increase in the basis of property sold by a taxpayer.

CHARITABLE REMAINDER ANNUITY TRUST   A *Charitable Remainder Annuity Trust* is a Trust that pays an annuity to a designated person (the Annuitant) for a certain period of time or until his death. Once the annuity is paid, whatever remains in the Trust is donated to a tax exempt charity.

CLAIM   A *claim* against the decedent's estate is a demand for payment. To be effective, the claim must be filed with the Probate court within the time limits set by law.

CLOSE CORPORATION A *Close Corporation* is a corporation whose voting shares are held by a single shareholder or a closely-knit group of shareholders.

CODICIL A *codicil* to a Will is an addition to the Will that changes or replaces certain parts of the Will.

COLUMBARIUM A *columbarium* is a vault with niches (spaces) for urns that contain the ashes of cremated bodies.

CORPORATION   A *Corporation* is a company created by one or more persons according to the laws of the state. The company is owned by the **shareholders** or **stockholders**. Each owner has limited liability (see Limited Liability).

CREDITOR   A *creditor* is someone to whom a debt is owed by another person (the *debtor*).

CUSTODIAN   A *Custodian* under the **Pennsylvania Uniform Gifts to Minors Act** is a financial institution or person who accepts responsibility for the care and management of property given to a minor child.

DEBTOR   A *debtor* is someone who owes payment of money or services to another person (the *creditor*).

DECEDENT   The *decedent* is the person who died.

DECLARANT   The *Declarant* is the person who signs an **Advance Directive For Health Care** in accordance with Pennsylvania law.

DESCENDANT   A *descendant* is someone who descends from a common ancestor. There are two kinds of descendants: a *lineal descendant* and a *collateral descendant*. The lineal descendant is one who descends in a straight line such as father to son to grandson. The collateral descendant is one who descends in a parallel line, such as a cousin. In this book, unless otherwise stated, the term *descendant* refers to a *lineal descendant*. The word *issue* has the same meaning as the word descendant.

DISTRIBUTION   The *distribution* of a Trust Estate or of a Probate Estate is the giving to the beneficiary that part of the Estate to which the beneficiary is entitled.

DURABLE As used in the Power of Attorney, the word *durable* means that the Power of Attorney will remain, in effect in the event that the principal (the person giving the Power of Attorney) becomes incapacitated.

ENTITLEMENT An *entitlement* is a right to receive some benefit income or property.

EQUITY INTEREST An *equity interest* is an ownership interest. It is the value of the ownership interest over and above monies owed on the property.

ESTATE A person's *Estate* is all of the property (both real and personal property) owned by that person. A person's estate is also referred to as his *Taxable Estate* because all of the decedent's assets must be included when determining whether any Estate taxes are due when the person dies. Compare to *Probate Estate*.

ELECTIVE SHARE The *Elective Share* is the minimum amount of the decedent's estate that a surviving spouse is entitled to receive under law. In Pennsylvania that amount is one third of the decedent's Estate.

EXECUTOR An *Executor* (or the feminine *Executrix*) refers to the person named in a Will to carry out the directions and requests given by the Will maker in that Will.

FACE VALUE The *face value* of a life insurance policy is the value stated on the insurance certificate or policy. It is the amount payable upon the death of the insured person.

FIDUCIARY A *Fiduciary* is one who takes on the duty of holding property in Trust for another or acting for the benefit of another. A Personal Representative, a Trustee, a Guardians are all considered to be fiduciaries. A fiduciary relationship is one of trust and confidence.

GLOSSARY *253*

GRANTEE The *Grantee* of a deed (also called the party of the second part) named in a deed is the person who receives title to the property from the Grantor.

GRANTOR A *Grantor* is someone who transfers property. The grantor of a deed, (also called the party of the first part), is the person who transfers property to a new owner (the *Grantee*). The Grantor of a Trust is someone who creates the Trust and then transfers property into the Trust. Also see *Settlor*.

GUARANTOR A *Guarantor* is someone who promises to pay a debt or perform a contract for another in the event that person does not fulfill his obligation.

GUARDIAN A *Guardian* is someone who has legal authority to care for the person or property of a minor or for someone who has been found by the court to be incapacitated.

HEALTH CARE SURROGATE   A *Health Care Surrogate* is a person appointed by someone (the Declarant) to make health care decisions for the Declarant in the event that he is too ill to speak for himself.

HEIR An *heir* is someone who is entitled to inherit the decedent's property in the event that the decedent dies without a Will. This includes the surviving spouse as well as the state of Pennsylvania, if the decedent had no surviving relative.

HOLOGRAPHIC WILL A *Holographic Will* is a Will written, dated and signed by the hand of the Will maker himself. Many states refuse to admit a Holographic Will into Probate unless it is witnessed according to the laws of the state.

HOMESTEAD The *homestead* is the dwelling that is owned, and occupied, in the state of Pennsylvania, as the owner's principal residence.

INCAPACITATED   The term *incapacitated* is used in two ways. A person is *physically incapacitated* if he lacks the ability to care for himself in some way. A person is *legally incapacitated* if a court finds that he is unable to care for his person or property.

IRREVOCABLE CONTRACT An *irrevocable contract* is a contract that cannot be revoked, withdrawn, or cancelled by any of the parties to that contract.

IRREVOCABLE TRUST   An *Irrevocable Trust* is a Trust that cannot be cancelled. It cannot be terminated until its purpose is accomplished.

IRREVOCABLE INSURANCE TRUST   An *Irrevocable Insurance Trust* is an irrevocable Trust that is set up to purchase life insurance. The proceeds of the life insurance policy can be used to pay taxes that may be due upon the death of the insured person.

JOINT TENANCY In Pennsylvania, a *Joint Tenancy* means that each tenant owns an equal share of the property. Those who are Joint Tenants of real property have no rights of survivorship unless the deed specifically says so.

KEY MAN INSURANCE *Key man insurance* is an insurance policy designed to protect a company from economic loss in the event that an important employee of the company becomes disabled or dies.

LAWS OF INTESTATE SUCCESSION The *Laws of Intestate Succession* are the laws of the state that determine who is to inherit the decedent's Probate Estate if the decedent died without a valid Will.

LEGALESE *Legalese* refers to the use of legal terms and confusing text used by many attorneys to draft legal documents.

LETTERS *Letters* is a document, issued by the Probate court, giving the Personal Representative authority to take possession of and to administer the Estate of the decedent.

LIEN A *lien* is a charge against a person's property as security for a debt. The lien is evidence of the creditor's right to take the property as full or partial payment, in the event that the debtor defaults in paying the monies owed.

LIFE ESTATE A *Life Estate* interest in real property is the right to possess and receive the income from that property for so long as the holder of the Life Estate lives. A 1/3rd Life Estate interest means the person can occupy 1/3rd of the property or receive 1/3rd of the income generated by that property.

LIMITED LIABILITY *Limited Liability* as related to a corporation or other company created according to state law, means that a shareholder of the company is not personally responsible to pay the debts of the company beyond the amount that he/she invested in the company.

LIMITED LIABILITY COMPANY   A *Limited Liability Company* is a company created according to the laws of the state, to conduct business or for any other lawful purpose. All of the members of the company have limited liability.

LIMITED PARTNERSHIP A *Limited Partnership* is a partnership created according to the laws of the state. Each *Limited Partner* has limited liability. Each *General Partner* is personally liable for all of the debts of the company. (See Limited Liability).

LITIGATION   *Litigation* is the process of carrying on a lawsuit, i.e., to sue for some right or remedy in a court of law. A Litigation Attorney is one who is experienced in conducting the law suit and in particular, going to trial.

LIVING WILL   A *Living Will* is an Advance Directive For Health Care that gives instructions to the physician about whether life support systems should be withheld or withdrawn in the event that the person who signs the Living Will is terminally ill or in a persistent vegetative state and unable to speak for himself.

MEDICAID   *Medicaid* is a public assistance program sponsored jointly by the federal and state government to provide medical care for people with low income and limited resources.

NET WORTH   A person's *net worth* is the value of all of the property that he owns less what he owes.

NEXT OF KIN   *Next of kin* has two meanings in law: *next of kin* can refer to a person's nearest blood relation or it can refer to those people (not necessarily blood relations) who are entitled to inherit the property of the decedent if the decedent died without a will.

GLOSSARY   *257*

NON-PROBATE TRANSFER A *Non-Probate Transfer* is a transfer made to a beneficiary of the decedent without going through a Probate procedure. This includes transfers from a joint account, a Trust, a Pay-On-Death or Transfer-On-Death account, etc.

PARTNERSHIP A business *partnership* is an agreement between two or more persons to use their assets and/or services to carry on a business for profit as co-owners.

PERSONAL EFFECTS *Personal effects* is property that is owned for one's personal use such as clothing, jewelry, books, and other items generally found in the one's home.

PERSONAL PROPERTY *Personal property* is all property owned by a person that is not real property (real estate). It includes personal effects, cars, securities, bank accounts, insurance policies, etc.

PERSONAL REPRESENTATIVE The *Personal Representative* is someone appointed by the Surrogate's Court to settle the decedent's estate and to distribute whatever is left to the proper beneficiary.

PETITION A *Petition* is a formal written, request to a Court asking the Court to take action or issue an order on a given matter; e.g. a request to appoint a Guardian.

POST-NUPTIAL AGREEMENT A *Post-nuptial agreement* is an agreement made by a couple after marriage to decide their respective rights in case of a dissolution or the death of a spouse.

POWER OF ATTORNEY A *Power of Attorney* is a document in which someone (the *Principal*) gives another (his *Agent*) authority to do specific things on behalf of the Principal.

PRENUPTIAL AGREEMENT   A *prenuptial agreement* (also known as an *antenuptial agreement*) is an agreement made prior to marriage whereby a couple determines how their property is to be managed during their marriage and how their property is to be divided should one die, or they later divorce.

PRINCIPAL OF A POWER OF ATTORNEY   The *Principal* of a Power of Attorney is someone who gives another (his *Agent*) authority to act on his (the Principal's) behalf.

PRINCIPAL OF A TRUST   The *Principal* of a Trust is the Trust property. The Trust income is the monies that are earned on the Trust Principal.

PROBABLE CAUSE   *Probable cause* exists if it is reasonable to believe certain facts. Mere suspicion is not enough. For probable cause to exist, there must be more evidence for the facts than against.

PROBATE   *Probate* is a Court procedure in which a Court determines the existence of a valid Will and then supervises the distribution of the Probate Estate of the decedent.

PROBATE ESTATE   The *Probate Estate* is that part of the decedent's Estate that is subject to Probate. It includes property that the decedent owned in his name only. It does not include property that was jointly held by the decedent and someone else. It does not include property held "in trust for" or "for the benefit of" someone.

PRO BONO   The term *Pro Bono* means "for the public good." When an attorney works Pro Bono, he does so voluntarily and without pay.

REAL PROPERTY   *Real property*, also known as *real estate*, is land and anything permanently attached to the land such as buildings and fences.

RESIDUARY BENEFICIARY A *residuary beneficiary* of a Will is a beneficiary who is entitled to whatever is left of the Probate Estate once the specific gifts made in the Will have been distributed and once the decedent's bills, taxes and costs of Probate have been paid. If there is more than one residuary beneficiary, then they all share equally in the residuary Estate, unless the Will provides for a different distribution.

RESOURCE   A *resource* for purposes of determining Medicaid eligibility, is an asset owned by the decedent, or his spouse, that can be converted to meet their needs. Federal statute 42 U.S.C. 1382b identifies what is (and is not) counted as a resource.

REVOCABLE LIVING TRUST   A *Revocable Living Trust* (also known as an *Inter Vivos Trust*) is a Trust that is created and becomes effective during the lifetime of the Settlor (or Grantor). A *revocable* Trust is one which can be amended or revoked by the Grantor or Settlor during his lifetime.

SELF PROVED WILL A *Self Proved Will* is a Will that eliminates some of the formalities of proof in a Probate procedure. The Will is made Self Proved by an Affidavit, signed by the witnesses, in the form as required by the statute.

SETTLOR A *Settlor* or a *Trustor* is someone who creates a Trust.

SOLE PROPRIETORSHIP   A *Sole Proprietorship* is a form of business ownership in which one person owns all of the assets of the business and that person is personally liable for all of the debts of the business

SPENDTHRIFT   A *Spendthrift* is someone who wastes money and/or spends lavishly.

SPENDTHRIFT TRUST   A *Spendthrift Trust* is a Trust created to provide monies for the living expenses of a beneficiary, and at the same time protect the monies from being taken by the creditors of the beneficiary.

STANDBY GUARDIAN   A *Standby Guardian* is someone appointed by a parent to take over the care of a child in the event that the parent becomes incapacitated or dies.

STEPPED-UP BASIS   A *stepped-up basis* is the value placed on property that is acquired in a transaction such as inheriting property or purchasing property. The "step-up" refers to the increase in value of basis from the basis of the former owner (usually what he paid for it), to the basis of the new owner (usually the market value when the transfer is made).

SURROGATE   A *surrogate* is a substitute; someone who acts in place of another. See Health Care Surrogate.

TENANCY BY THE ENTIRETY   A *Tenancy by the Entirety* is the name of a form of ownership of real property held by a husband and wife. It is a joint tenancy with right of survivorship, modified by the common law theory that the husband and wife are one. With a joint tenancy with right of survivor, each joint tenant owns their own share of the property until death, when the surviving owner owns it 100%. With a Tenancy by the Entirety, each owns 100% of the property both before and after death.

TENANCY IN COMMON   *Tenancy in common* is a form of ownership such that each tenant owns his/her share without any claim to that share by the other tenants. Unlike a joint tenancy, there is no right of survivorship. Once a tenant in common dies, his/her share belongs to the tenant's estate and not to the remaining owners of the property.

TITLE INSURANCE   *Title Insurance* is a policy issued by a title company after searching title to the property. The insurance covers losses that result from a defect of title, such as unpaid taxes, or someone with a claim of ownership of the property.

TRUST AGREEMENT A *Trust Agreement* is a document in which someone (the Grantor or Settlor) creates a Trust and appoints a Trustee to manage property placed into the Trust. The usual purpose of the Trust is to benefit persons or charities named by the Grantor as beneficiaries of the Trust.

TRUSTEE   A *Trustee* is a person, or institution, who accepts the duty of caring for property for the benefit of another.

UNDUE INFLUENCE   *Undue influence* is pressure, influence or persuasion that overpowers a person's free will or judgment, so that a person acts according to the will or purpose of the dominating party.

VOID PROVISION   A *void provision* is one that is not legally enforceable. For example, if a Will provision makes a gift and the Court finds that provision to be void, then the beneficiary has no legal right to receive that gift.

WAIVER   A *waiver* is the intentional and voluntary giving up of a known right.

INDEX

A

ABSTRACT OF TITLE 232

ACCOUNTING 24, 126, 128, 176

ADOPTED CHILD 13

ADMINISTRATION
Ancillary 37
Full 22-24
Small Estate 18

ADULT CHILD 134

ADVANCE DIRECTIVE
168, 171, 182, 239, 244

AFFIDAVIT 19, 20, 181

AFTERBORN CHILD 10, 241

AGENT 178-183

ANATOMICAL GIFT
130, 164, 165, 169

ANCILLARY ADMIN. 37

ANNUAL GIFT TAX EXCLUSION
53, 109

ANNUITIES 89-91, 142-149
196, 231

APPEAL, MEDICAID 224-228

APPRAISAL 23, 234

ARTIFICIAL INSEMINATION 10

ATTORNEY FEE 23, 49, 126, 176

ATTORNEY IN FACT 178

AUTOMOBILE, Exempt 197

AUTOPSY 130, 165-167, 169

B

BANK ACCOUNTS
Agency 174
Beneficiary 29, 66
Funeral 198
Held in Trust 30, 43, 44, 158
Joint 26, 50, 72, 174, 199
Patient Care 19
Pay on Death
30, 41, 50, 59, 69

BANKRUPTCY 92

BASIS, Step-up 58, 216

BENEFICIARY
Account 29, 66
Of Insurance 87-90
Of Pension 90, 231
Of Trust 46, 52, 69, 134
Residuary 66, 68, 138

BIGAMY 9

BOND 24, 175, 176

263

BURIAL
   Arrangements   153, 198
   Military   156
   Site   153

BUSINESS,
   Debts   98, 100, 114
   Estate Plan   99
   Insurance   104
   Partnership   101

BY REPRESENTATION   16

C

CAPITAL GAINS TAX
   39, 54, 58, 114, 116, 117
   141-149, 216, 219, 233

CAR LOAN   85, 201

CAREGIVER   135, 136, 222

CEMETERIES, National   156

CENTERS FOR MEDICARE &
   MEDICAID SERVICES 190, 218

CHALLENGING A WILL   72-74

CHARITABLE TRUST   141-149

CHILD
   Adopted   13
   Adult   134
   Afterborn   10, 241
   Disabled   135-138, 202
      213, 222
   Minor   70, 120-129
      136, 213, 222
   Nonmarital   14
   Stepchild   130-132
   Trust for   129, 132

CLERK OF THE COURT   8

CODICIL   240

COLUMBARIUM   155

COMMON LAW MARRIAGE   9

COMMUNITY SPOUSE
   192-204, 220

CORPORATE VEIL   106

CORPORATION   107, 108

COURT   6-10, 20, 22-24, 45-47
   49, 50, 52, 69, 72
   74-76, 121-126, 176, 183

CREDIT CARD DEBT   84, 201

CREDITOR
   Claim   23, 46, 47
   Notifying   24
   Protection   47, 50, 89-90
      93, 149, 244

CREMATION   154

CUSTODIAN   126-129

D

DEBTS
   Business   98, 100, 114
   Credit Card   87, 201
   Joint   82, 84, 87
   Payment of   68
   Spouse   82

DESCENDANT   15, 17

DEEDS	32-34
DISABLED CHILD	135-138, 213 202, 222
DISCRETIONARY TRUST	138
DIVORCE	239
DOCTRINE OF NECESSARIES	80
DONOR CARD	164
DOWER RIGHTS	36
DURABLE POWER OF ATTORNEY	178, 183

E
ELECTIVE SHARE	50
ERRORS & OMISSIONS	104
ESTATE TAX	37, 53-58, 111 114-116, 143, 196, 216, 246
ESTATE PLAN	
For Business	90
For Health Care	168
EXEMPT RESOURCES	197-200
EXCLUSION AMOUNT	53, 56
EXEMPT PROPERTY	90, 91

F
FAIR HEARING	226
FAMILY	
Business	100, 111
Exemption	90
Partnership	109-111
Trust	134
FEDERAL RETIREE	231
FICTIOUS NAME	100
FUNERAL, Pre-Need	157-161, 198

G
GENERAL PARTNER	108-110
GIFT	
Prior	67
Specific	65, 66
Tax	53, 54, 56, 109, 148, 216
To Minor	125-129
GRANTEE OF DEED	32, 34, 35
GRANTOR	
of Deed	32
of Trust	43, 47, 53
GUARANTOR	82, 103
GUARDIAN	
Appointing	48, 70, 78, 121 135, 136, 171, 183, 220
Avoiding	47, 175
Fees	176
Standby	121-123

H
HALF BLOOD	16

INDEX *265*

HEALTH CARE
   Advance Directive
      168, 171, 182, 239, 244
   Estate Plan   173
   Paying for   184-188
   Surrogate
      168, 169 177, 182, 244

HOLOGRAPHIC WILL   71

HOMESTEAD
   Exempt Resource   197
   Gift Of   38, 68, 215-223
   Protection   220-223

I

INCAPACITATED   135-138, 181

INCOME
   Cap   245
   Tax   109, 110, 148

INHERITANCE TAX
        35, 37, 56, 57, 69

INSURANCE
   Annuities
     89-91, 142-149, 196, 231
   Business   104
   Errors & Omissions   104
   Key man   105, 114
   Life   20, 66, 69, 84
      87-90, 94, 114, 116
      125, 127, 132, 198
   Loan   85, 86
   Long term care   185-189
   Mortgage   85
   Term   125, 198
   Title   231, 232

INTER VIVOS TRUST   42-54, 136

IN TERROREM   74

INTESTATE SUCCESSION (See Laws
    of Intestate Succession)

IN TRUST FOR ACCT   5, 30, 41

INVENTORY 24, 76, 126, 175, 176

IRA ACCOUNT   66, 91, 93, 199

IRREVOCABLE
   Charitable Trust   147
   Contract   160
   Gift   127
   Insurance Trust   116, 117
   Pre-need Funeral   160, 198
   Trust   44, 134, 147, 217

J

JOINT
   Bank Account   26, 50, 66
              72, 174, 199
   Credit Card   84, 201
   Debts   82, 84, 87
   Property   5, 25, 26, 30, 31
       37, 41, 66, 83, 199
   Tenant   30-33, 35-38, 83
   Trust   54

K

KEOGH ACCOUNT   93

KEYS   230, 248

KEY MAN INSURANCE   105, 114

L

LAWS OF INTESTATE SUCCESSION
                        2, 5, 7, 11, 13-17
                        33, 67, 243

LAWYER, how to find   xi-xiii

LEGAL SERVICES   xii, 136

LIFE
  Estate   34, 35, 38, 218, 219
  Expectancy   115, 142, 218
  Insurance   20, 66, 69, 84
                      87-90, 94, 114, 116
                      125, 127, 132, 198

LIMITED
  Liability Company   112, 113
  Partnership   108-111
  Power of Attorney   179, 180

LIVING TRUST   42-54

LIVING WILL   168, 170

LOAN INSURANCE   85, 86

LONG TERM CARE   184-188

LOOK BACK PERIOD   207

M

MARRIAGE   8, 9, 240, 241

MARRIED WOMAN'S RTS   80

MEDICAID
  Appeal   195, 224-228
  Burial Arrangements   198
  Community Spouse   192
  Eligibility   191
  Exempt Resources   196-199
  Fair Hearing   226
  Home   197, 213-224
  Income   192, 245
  Lien   213, 220
  Look back   207
  Medical Eligibility   191
  Min. Need Allow.   195, 196
  Penalty Period   203-208
                      219, 223
  Personal Needs Allow.   192
  Recipient   192, 193
  Resource Allowance   194
  Rule of Halves   205, 206
  Shelter Allowance   195
  Spend-down   200, 201
  Snap-shot Date   201
  Uncomp. Transfer   204

MEDICARE COVERAGE   184

MILITARY BURIAL   156

MINOR CHILD   70, 120-129
                  136, 213, 222

MINIMUM NEED ALLOWANCE
                        195, 196

MORTGAGE INSUR.   85, 87

MOTOR VEHICLE   21, 198

N

NARFE 186

NET WORTH 4

NEXT OF KIN
 17, 65, 151, 169, 233

NON-PROBATE ASSET
 19, 50, 66, 69

NONMARITAL CHILD 14

O

OFFICE OF PERSONAL
 MANAGEMENT 231

OFFSHORE TRUST 94-98

OPERATING AGREEMENT 112

ORGAN DONOR CARD 164

ORPHAN'S COURT
 6-8, 22, 52, 107

OUT OF STATE PROPERTY
 36, 37

OVERWEIGHT 155

P

PACEMAKER 154

PAY ON DEATH ACCOUNT
 30, 41, 50, 59, 69

PARTNERSHIP AGREEMENT
 105, 132

PATIENT CARE ACCOUNT 19

PENALTY PERIOD
 203-208, 219, 223

PENNSYLVANIA
 Agencies
  See STATE AGENCIES
 Statutes See STATUTES
 Web sites See WEB SITES

PENSION 90, 231

PERSONAL
 Effects 65, 197
 Needs Allowance 192
 Property 65, 197, 234

PERSONAL REPRESENTATIVE
 Appoint 20, 63, 78
 Duties 23, 51, 65
  76, 107, 233
 Fee 23, 45, 63, 64

PETITION 10, 18, 121-123, 175

PETS 139, 140

POUR OVER WILL 51

POWER OF ATTORNEY
 177-183, 239

PRE-NEED FUNERAL PLAN
 152, 157-161, 198

PRENUPTIAL AGREEMENT
 132, 133, 235, 241

PROBABLE CAUSE 74

PROBATE
Avoiding 38, 45
Cost of 18, 24, 38, 129, 148
Court see COURT
Estate 6, 15, 16, 23, 24
47, 51, 66, 82, 90

PRINCIPAL 178

PROPERTY
Joint 5, 25, 26, 30, 31
37, 41, 66, 83, 199
Held in Trust 5, 41, 43, 44
Out of State 36, 37

Q
QUICK FIND FOLDER 236-238

R
REAL PROPERTY 32-37, 199

RECORDS
Court 47
Organizing 230
Personal 234
Tax 233

REGISTER OF WILLS 6, 22

REMAINDER INTEREST
34, 218, 219. 221

RESIDUARY
Beneficiary 66, 68, 139

RESOURCE
Allowance 194-196
Exempt 196-199

REVOCABLE LIVING TRUST
42-54, 107

RIGHT OF SURVIVOR
26, 32, 36, 37, 41, 83

S
SAFE DEPOSIT BOX
75-77, 230, 248

SAME SEX MARRIAGE 9

SECURITIES 31, 50, 51

SELF-PROVED WILL 71

SETTLOR 43

SHELTER ALLOWANCE 195

SSI 160, 191, 217

SNAP-SHOT DATE 201

SOLE PROPRIETORSHIP
100, 102-104

SPECIAL NEEDS TRUST 137, 222

SPECIFIC GIFT 65, 66

SPEND DOWN 200

SPENDTHRIFT TRUST 46

SPOUSE 7-9, 82, 90

SPRINGING POWER ATTY 181

STANDBY GUARDIAN 121-123

STATE AGENCIES (Pennsylvania)
  County Assistance Office 190
  Dept. of Aging 185
  Dept. of Public Transportation
    (PENNDOT) 21
  Dept. of Public Welfare
    19, 160, 190
  Dept. of Revenue 76, 144
  Dept. of State 102, 103
  Human Gifts Registry 164
  Office of Medical
    Assistance Programs 190
  Register of Wills 22
  Secretary of State 112
  State Bd. Funeral Dir. 159

STATUTES, FEDERAL

  CODE OF FED. REGULATIONS
  16 CFR 453.3 154
  42 CFR 430-435 224
  42 CFR 433.36 213
  42 CFR 435.541 191
  42 CFR 435.908 191

  INTERNAL REVENUE CODE
  IRC 501 142
  IRC 1022 58
  IRC 2503 53

  UNITED STATES CODE
  42 U.S.C. 1382 137, 193, 197
  42 U.S.C. 1396a 213
  42 U.S.C 1396p 137, 206
    214, 221, 222
  42 U.S.C 1396r 194, 202

STATUTES, PENNSYLVANIA

  PENNSYLVANIA CODE OF
    REGULATIONS (Pa.Code)
  49 / 13.226 58
  55 / 125.84 191
  55 / 141.81 191
  55 / 178.2 198
  55 / 178.4 192, 199
  55 / 178.5 160, 198
  55 / 178.22 197
  55 / 178.51 199
  55 / 178.64 199
  55 / 178.65 199
  55 / 178.67 198
  55 / 178.69 198
  55 / 178.70 198
  55 / 178.71 198
  55 / 178.73 198
  55 / 178.91 199
  55 / 178.104
    206, 214, 221, 222
  55 / 178.174 199, 206
  55 / 181.452 192
  55 / 275.1 226
  55 / 275.4 226
  55 / 1101.92 207
  55 / 1101.93 207

  PENNSYLVANIA STATUTES (P.S.)
  7 P.S. 605 30
  7 P.S. 609 174
  9 P.S. 201 153
  21 P.S. 82 80
  35 P.S. 1111 169
  62 P.S. 446 191
  63 P.S. 480.5 159
  68 P.S. 110 33

STATUTES, PENNSYLVANIA (P.S.)
72 P.S. 1895	102
72 P.S. 7301	143
72 P.S. 7403	102
72 P.S. 9107	57
72 P.S. 9116	57
72 P.S. 9117	55
72 P.S. 9126	57
72 P.S. 9130	57
72 P.S. 9142	57

PENNSYLVANIA CONSOLIDATED STATUTES (Pa.C.S.)
7 Pa.C.S 604	26
20 Pa.C.S. 921	47
20 Pa.C.S. 7121	52

PENNSYLVANIA CONSOLIDATED STATUTES ANNOTATED
Pa.C.S.A
15 / 153	102
15 / 8511	108
15 / 8523	108
15 / 8533	108
15 / 8564	110
15 / 8911	112
15 / 8914	112
15 / 8922	112
15 / 8924	112
15 / 8941	112
20 / 305	153
20 / 2102	15
20 / 2103	17
20 / 2104	10, 16, 17
20 / 2107	14
20 /2203	50
20 / 2505	240
20/ 2507	241
20 / 2514	68

Pa.C.S.A
20 /2515	51
20 / 2519	70, 121
20 / 2521	74
20 / 3101	19, 20, 240
20 / 3102	18
20 / 3121	90
20 / 3132.1	71
20 / 3155	63
20 / 3162	23
20 / 3301	23
20 / 3385	23
20 / 3392	90
20 / 3501.1	23
20 / 3507	239
20 / 3532	23
20 / 3537	23
20 / 3702	69
20 / 3704	69
20 / 3706	69
20 / 5101	125
20 / 5103	125
20 / 5113	124
20 / 5115	136
20 / 5121	136
20 / 5142	126, 175
20 / 5146	136
20 / 5161	126
20 / 5304	127
20 / 5307	125
20 / 5309	127
20 / 5311	127
20 / 5321	127
20 / 5310	129
20 / 5314	128
20 / 5315	128
20 / 5319	128
20 / 5404	168

PENNSYLVANIA CONSOLIDATED
STATUTES ANNOTATED

Pa.C.S.A
20 / 5511	47, 175
20 / 5512.1	175
20 / 5514	135, 136
20 / 5515	136
20 / 5516	175
20 / 5518	175
20 / 5521	176
20 / 5601.1	178
20 / 5602	178
20 / 5603	178, 178
20 / 5606	181
20 / 5702	183
20 / 6111.1	239
20 / 6111.2	239
20 / 6112	46
20 / 6114	13
20 / 6304	30, 66, 83
20 / 6402	31
20 / 6407	31
20 / 6410	31
20 / 7185	49
20 / 8611	165
20 / 8613	164
20 / 8619	164
23 / 1102	8
23 / 1103	9
23 / 1301	8
23 / 1304	8
23 / 1702	9
23 / 1703	8
23 / 3304	9
23 / 5603	123
23 / 5611	122

Pa.C.S.A
23 / 5613	123
23 / 5614	123
42 / 931	6
42 / 951	6
42 / 8124	87, 89, 90, 91, 94
42 / 9124	93
54 / 303	100
54 / 311	100
72 / 9192	76
72 / 9193	76
72 / 9144	69

STEPCHILD   130-132

STEP-UP IN BASIS 58, 216, 233

SUCCESSOR TRUSTEE   43-53
                  129, 133, 179

SURROGATE CONTRACT
                        12, 13

T

TAXABLE ESTATE   53, 56

TAX
  Apportionment   69
  Capital Gains
    39, 54, 58, 114, 116, 117
    141-149, 216, 219, 233
  Estate   37, 53-58, 111
    114-116, 143, 196, 216, 246
  Gift   53, 54, 56
    109, 148, 216
  Income   109, 110, 148
  Inheritance
    35, 37, 56, 57, 69

A Will is Not Enough in Pennsylvania

TENANTS BY THE ENTIRETY
  33, 35, 239

TENANTS IN COMMON
  33, 35, 37, 51, 83, 221, 239

TERM INSURANCE   125, 198

TITLE INSURANCE   231, 232

TOD SECURITY   31, 50, 51

TRANSFERS
  Non-probate   19
  Of Home   214-223
  Of Motor Vehicle   21
  Of Real Property   32-37
  Of Securities   31, 50, 51
  Out of State   36, 37
  To Disabled Child   136, 222
  To Minor   120-129, 222

TRUST
  Account   30, 44, 158
  Charitable   141-149
  Discretionary   138
  Family   134
  For Child   70, 132
  For Pet   139
  Inter Vivos   42
  Irrevocable   116, 117, 147
  Joint   54
  Offshore   94-98
  Property   5, 41, 43, 44
  Revocable Living   42-54, 107
  Second Marriage   133
  Special Needs   136, 137, 222
  Spendthrift   46

TRUSTEE   43-49, 52
                   70, 133, 149

TRUSTOR   43

U

UNDUE INFLUENCE   71-73

UNIFORM TRANSFERS
  TO MINORS   126-129

UNCOMPENSATED TRANSFER
                           204

V

VETERAN'S ADMIN.   156

W

WAGES   19

WEB SITES
  Federal Statutes   viii
  Office of Med. Assist.   190
  PA Bar Assoc.   xi
  PA Statutes   viii
  NARFE   186
  US Office Personnel Mgmt
                            185
  Veteran's Cemetery   156

WILL
  Challenge   72
  Codicil   240
  Holographic   71
  Pour-over   51
  Prepare   71
  Revoke   240
  Self-proved   71
  Store   75

INDEX *273*

143 Pennsylvania laws and regulations are referenced in
A Will Is Not Enough In Pennsylvania

Each state has its own set of laws relating to the control, and protection of a person's Estate. The Pennsylvania laws relating to Guardianship, Probate and especially Medicaid are very different from the laws of other states.

The author is in the process of "translating" *A Will Is Not Enough* for the rest of the states; that is, to write a book that incorporates the laws of the state into a book that describes how to prepare an Estate Plan appropriate to the given state.

A Will Is Not Enough is now available for:
CALIFORNIA, FLORIDA, MARYLAND, MICHIGAN
NEW JERSEY, NEW YORK, OREGON
PENNSYLVANIA, TEXAS and VIRGINIA

To check whether this book is currently available for other states call Eagle Publishing Company of Boca at
(800) 824-0823
or visit our Web site http://www.eaglepublishing.com

SPECIAL OFFER FOR PURCHASERS OF THIS BOOK
$25 INCLUDES SHIPPING

Guiding Those Left Behind

Amelia E. Pohl has written a series of books explaining how to settle an Estate. Each book is state specific, telling how things are done in that state. Each book explains:
- ✧ who to notify
- ✧ how to locate the decedent's property
- ✧ how to get possession of the inheritance
- ✧ when you do, and do not, need an attorney
- ✧ the rights of a beneficiary, and much more.

Each book is written with the assistance of an experienced attorney who is licensed and is practicing in that state.

The *Guiding* series is currently available for the following states: ALABAMA, ARIZONA, CALIFORNIA, FLORIDA
GEORGIA, ILLINOIS, INDIANA, KENTUCKY
MASSACHUSETTS, MARYLAND, MICHIGAN,
MINNESOTA, MISSOURI, NEW JERSEY, NEW YORK
NORTH CAROLINA, OHIO, PENNSYLVANIA
SOUTH CAROLINA, TENNESSEE, TEXAS, VIRGINIA
WASHINGTON, WISCONSIN

Mississippi, Connecticut and Hawaii are scheduled for release in 2003.

Visit our Web site http://www.eaglepublishing.com
to check whether books for other states are available at this time.

SPECIAL OFFER FOR PURCHASERS OF THIS BOOK
$22 INCLUDES SHIPPING

To order call (800) 824-0823

BOOK REVIEWS FOR GUIDING THOSE LEFT BEHIND

ARIZONA

Ben T. Traywick of the Tombstone Epitaph said "This book is an excellent reference book that simplifies all the necessary tasks that must be done when there is a death in the family. There is even an explanation as to how you can arrange your own estate so that your heirs will not be left with a multitude of nagging problems." "This reviewer has been going through probate for two years with no end yet in sight. This book at the beginning, two years ago, would have helped immensely."

CALIFORNIA

Margot Petit Nichols of the Carmel Pine Cone called it a "...TRULY RIVETING READ." "... I could scarcely put it down." "This is a book that we should all have, either on our book shelves or thoughtfully placed with our important papers."

FLORIDA

Maryhelen Clague of the Tampa Tribune Times wrote "Amelia Pohl has created a handy, self-help guide that illustrates the necessary steps that must be taken when someone dies, a guide that is easy to read, extremely clear and simple to refer to when the need arises."

TEXAS

Lois Scott of the Victoria Advocate wrote "I think this is a most valuable book that each family should have on hand. One never knows when it might be needed suddenly."

It is the goal of EAGLE PUBLISHING COMPANY to keep our publications fresh.

As we receive information about changes to the federal or Pennsylvania law we will post an update to this edition at our Web site:

        http://www.eaglepublishing.com